VANUATU TRAVEL GUIDE

2024 Edition

Discovering Paradise: Dive into a World of Culture, Adventure, and Natural Beauty and Uncover the Hidden Gems of the South Pacific Archipelago

By

Roy McKean

TABLE OF CONTENT

CHAPTER THREE

MUST VISIT DESTINATIONS

CHAPTER FOUR

NAVIGATING VANUATU

CHAPTER FIVE

ACCOMMODATION

5.1 HOTELS AND RESORTS

5.2 BOUTIQUE STAYS

5.3 BUDGET-FRIENDLY OPTIONS

5.4 UNIQUE ACCOMMODATION EXPERIENCES

5.5 BOOKING ACCOMMODATION IN ADVANCE

CHAPTER SIX

DINING IN VANUATU

6.1 MUST-TASTE DISHES AND LOCAL DELICACIES

6.2 INTERNATIONAL FLAVORS

6.3 LOCAL MARKET ADVENTURES

6.4 DINING ETIQUETTE

6.5 RECOMMENDED RESTAURANTS WITH THEIR LOCATIONS

CHAPTER SEVEN

ENTERTAINMENT AND NIGHTLIFE

7.1 NIGHTCLUBS AND LOUNGES WITH THEIR LOCATIONS

7.1.1 Club Tropicana: A Night of Energetic Revelry in the Heart of Port Vila

7.1.2 Volcano Vibes Lounge: Where Relaxation Meets Excitement on Tanna Island

7.1.3 Harbor Lights Club: Dancing Beneath the Stars in Luganville, Espiritu Santo

7.1.4 Mystique Lounge: Discovering Intimacy and Sophistication in Port Olry, Espiritu Santo

7.2 FAMILY-FRIENDLY ENTERTAINMENT

CHAPTER EIGHT

CULTURAL EXPERIENCES

CHAPTER NINE

OUTDOOR ACTIVITIES

CHAPTER TEN

VANUATU TRAVEL ITINERARIES

CHAPTER ELEVEN

PRACTICAL TIPS AND RESOURCES

DISCLAIMER

Welcome to our immersive travel guide! As you embark on this journey through the pages of Vanuatu travel guide, we want to set clear expectations. While we aim to transport you to captivating destinations and provide valuable insights, we do so without the aid of maps and images.

Why, you ask?

Our intention is simple: to stimulate your imagination and curiosity. By omitting maps, we encourage you to rely on your instincts, engage with locals, and discover hidden gems beyond the well-trodden paths. Instead of images, we invite you to paint vivid mental pictures through words and descriptions, allowing your mind to craft its unique interpretation of the places we explore.

In this text-centric guide, we prioritize storytelling, history, culture, and practical advice. We believe that your own perceptions and interpretations will make your travels more personal and memorable. It's an invitation to be present in the moment, to interact with your surroundings, and to embrace the serendipitous adventures that come your way.

So, as you delve into these pages, let your imagination soar, and let the words be your compass in this world of exploration and discovery.

INTRODUCTION

Welcome to Vanuatu

Welcome to Vanuatu, a captivating jewel cradled in the South Pacific. This archipelago, comprising 83 islands, invites travelers into a realm of unparalleled natural beauty, vibrant cultures, and unparalleled warmth. Azure blue waters, flourishing rainforests, and a kaleidoscope of marine life converge to create a haven for those seeking an authentic and immersive travel experience.

Vanuatu's allure lies in its diverse landscapes. From the dynamic volcanoes of Tanna to the unspoiled beaches of Espiritu Santo, each island offers a distinctive and awe-inspiring vista. Immerse yourself in crystal-clear waters alive with marine wonders, traverse dense jungles echoing with the sounds of exotic birds, and witness the dramatic beauty of cascading waterfalls.

The cultural tapestry of Vanuatu is woven with the rich traditions of its indigenous people. With a profound history of tribal customs and ceremonies, visitors are welcomed to engage with local communities, partake in traditional dances, and gain insight into a unique way of life that has been lovingly preserved for generations.

For the adventurous soul, Vanuatu is a playground of possibilities. Dive enthusiasts can explore world-class dive sites, hikers can meander through scenic trails in lush landscapes, and those seeking tranquility can find solace on secluded beaches. Yet, beyond the adrenaline and picturesque landscapes, the true treasure of Vanuatu lies in its people. Warm smiles and genuine hospitality accompany visitors at every turn. The Ni-Vanuatu, proud of their cultural heritage, eagerly share their traditions with those who venture to their shores.

Vanuatu possesses a unique spirit that transcends postcard-perfect scenes. Here, time seems to slow down, inviting visitors to connect with the natural surroundings and immerse themselves in a tranquil and unspoiled environment.

Whether you yearn for relaxation on pristine beaches, cultural immersion with indigenous communities, or thrilling adventures in the great outdoors, Vanuatu extends an invitation to discover a paradise like no other. Pack your sense of adventure and prepare to explore the wonders that await in this Pacific gem. Welcome to Vanuatu, where every moment is an invitation to create memories that will last a lifetime.

Why Vanuatu?

Natural Beauty: Vanuatu is a visual feast for nature lovers. From the active volcanoes of Tanna to the pristine beaches of Espiritu Santo, each island offers a distinctive and awe-inspiring landscape. Dive into crystal-clear waters teeming with marine life, explore dense jungles, and witness the breathtaking beauty of cascading waterfalls.

Cultural Riches: The cultural tapestry of Vanuatu is woven with the traditions of its indigenous people. With a rich history of tribal customs and ceremonies, visitors have the opportunity to engage with local communities, participate in traditional dances, and gain insight into the unique way of life that has been preserved for generations.

Adventure Awaits: Whether you're a thrill-seeker or a laid-back explorer, Vanuatu has something for everyone. Dive enthusiasts can explore world-class dive sites, hikers can traverse scenic trails through lush landscapes, and those seeking relaxation can bask in the serenity of secluded beaches.

Friendly Locals: One of the greatest treasures of Vanuatu is its people. Warm smiles and genuine hospitality greet visitors at every turn. The locals, known as Ni-Vanuatu, are proud of their cultural heritage and are eager to share it with those who venture to their shores.

Vanuatu's Unique Spirit: Beyond the postcard-perfect scenes, there's a distinct spirit that sets Vanuatu apart. It's a place where time seems to slow down, allowing visitors to connect with the natural surroundings and immerse themselves in a tranquil and unspoiled environment.

Whether you seek relaxation on pristine beaches, cultural immersion with indigenous communities, or thrilling adventures in the great outdoors, Vanuatu invites you to discover a paradise like no other. So, pack your sense of adventure and get ready to explore the wonders that await in this Pacific gem. Welcome to Vanuatu, where every moment is an invitation to create memories that will last a lifetime.

CHAPTER ONE

PLANNING YOUR VANUATU ADVENTURE

1.1 Setting Your Travel Goals

Embarking on a journey to Vanuatu is an exciting prospect, promising a tapestry of experiences that range from tranquil beach retreats to heart-pounding outdoor adventures. However, to make the most of your Vanuatu adventure, it is paramount to begin with a clear definition of your travel goals. This initial step not only sets the tone for your entire journey but also serves as the compass guiding you through the diverse offerings of this Pacific paradise.

Defining Your Travel Goals: Crafting the Blueprint for Your Adventure

Every traveler is unique, and so are their aspirations. Some yearn for the soothing embrace of pristine beaches, where turquoise waters gently lap against the shore, and coconut palms sway in the breeze. Others are drawn to the cultural heartbeat of a destination, seeking immersive experiences that connect them with the traditions, rituals, and daily lives of the local population. Meanwhile, adventure enthusiasts crave the thrill of exploration, eager to conquer volcanic landscapes, dive into vibrant coral reefs, and trek through lush rainforests.

By taking the time to pinpoint your travel goals, you lay the foundation for a tailored and fulfilling Vanuatu experience.

Are you dreaming of lazy days on the beach, sipping coconut water as the sun sets over the horizon? Or does the idea of mingling with local communities, participating in traditional ceremonies, and savoring indigenous cuisines captivate your imagination? Perhaps it's the adrenaline rush of hiking to hidden waterfalls, diving into underwater caves, or witnessing the power of an active volcano that fuels your wanderlust.

Relaxation on Pristine Beaches: The Beach Bum's Delight

For those seeking relaxation, Vanuatu boasts an array of idyllic beaches that seem plucked from a postcard. Imagine stretches of powdery white sand meeting the crystal-clear waters of the Pacific. Whether it's basking in the sun, enjoying water sports, or simply strolling along the shoreline, the beaches of Vanuatu offer a tranquil haven for relaxation enthusiasts.

Cultural Immersion: Connecting with the Heartbeat of Vanuatu

Vanuatu's rich cultural tapestry invites travelers to immerse themselves in a world where traditions are cherished, and community bonds run deep. From engaging in ancient ceremonies to learning traditional dance forms, cultural immersion in Vanuatu provides a profound understanding of the local way of life. By defining cultural exploration as a key goal, your journey becomes a vibrant mosaic of shared moments and cross-cultural connections.

Thrilling Outdoor Activities: Adrenaline-Pumping Adventures Await

For the thrill-seekers, Vanuatu is a playground of adventure. Picture yourself standing on the rim of an active volcano, feeling the earth beneath you rumble. Envision diving into the technicolor world beneath the waves, exploring coral reefs teeming with marine life. By setting thrilling outdoor activities as your goal, you transform your Vanuatu adventure into an adrenaline-fueled escapade, filled with awe-inspiring moments and daring exploits.

1.2 Choosing the Best Time to Visit

Embarking on a journey to Vanuatu is not just about reaching a destination; it's about experiencing a symphony of climates, each playing its own seasonal melody. To truly optimize your visit to this South Pacific archipelago, it's essential to delve into the nuances of Vanuatu's diverse climates and uncover the seasonal highlights that make each period unique. By strategically planning your trip, you can immerse yourself in the magic of local festivals, revel in ideal weather conditions, and witness extraordinary natural phenomena that define the essence of Vanuatu.

Understanding Vanuatu's Diverse Climates: A Journey Through the Seasons

Vanuatu, comprised of 83 islands, showcases a remarkable diversity of climates, ranging from tropical to subtropical. The archipelago experiences two distinct seasons: the wet season, from November to April, and the dry season, from May to October. Each season brings its own set of characteristics, offering travelers a choice of atmospheres to tailor their visit.

The Wet Season: November to April

The wet season in Vanuatu is characterized by higher temperatures, increased humidity, and occasional heavy rainfall. While the rainforest landscapes flourish, creating lush, vibrant scenes, the wet season also coincides with the occurrence of tropical cyclones. Travelers should be mindful of this when planning their visit during these months. However, the wet season is not without its perks. It is an ideal time for those seeking lush, green landscapes, and it's the season when waterfalls cascade in full force, creating breathtaking natural spectacles.

The Dry Season: May to October

The dry season, on the other hand, is marked by cooler temperatures and lower humidity. This is generally considered the best time to visit Vanuatu, as the weather is more predictable, and the risk of cyclones diminishes. During the dry season, the islands boast clear skies, making it an excellent time for outdoor activities such as hiking, snorkeling, and exploring the diverse landscapes. The visibility for underwater adventures is at its peak, making it a favorite among diving enthusiasts.

Strategically Planning Your Trip: Aligning with Seasonal Highlights

Local Festivals: Vanuatu is known for its vibrant and diverse festivals, each offering a unique cultural experience. By aligning your visit with local festivities, you can immerse yourself in the rich traditions and celebrations that define the identity of each island. From the Land Diving Festival on Pentecost to the Toka Festival on Tanna, these events provide an authentic glimpse into the cultural tapestry of Vanuatu.

Ideal Weather Conditions: The dry season, with its clear skies and milder temperatures, is ideal for those seeking outdoor adventures and beach escapades. Whether you're hiking through the dense jungles of Espiritu Santo or lounging on the white sands of Mystery Island, the dry season offers optimal weather conditions for a wide range of activities.

Natural Phenomena: Vanuatu is home to awe-inspiring natural wonders that come to life during specific seasons. Witnessing the majestic Yasur Volcano on Tanna, exploring the underwater caves of Espiritu Santo, or encountering the unique land divers of Pentecost are experiences that can be enhanced by understanding the seasonal nuances and planning your visit accordingly.

In essence, strategically planning your trip to Vanuatu involves more than just booking flights and accommodations. It's about aligning your visit with the rhythm of the islands, tapping into the magic of local festivals, embracing ideal weather conditions, and immersing yourself in the natural phenomena that make Vanuatu a unique and captivating destination. By understanding the diverse climates and seasonal highlights, you can orchestrate a symphony of experiences that resonate with the very soul of this Pacific paradise. So, whether you're drawn to the lushness of the wet season or the clarity of the dry season, let the seasons of Vanuatu guide you on a journey of discovery and wonder.

1.3 Visa and Entry Requirements

Traveling to Vanuatu, the jewel of the South Pacific, is a dream come true for many adventure-seekers, beach enthusiasts, and culture lovers. However, before you can bask in the turquoise waters and explore the lush landscapes, it's crucial to navigate the intricacies of Vanuatu's visa and entry requirements. This comprehensive guide provides all the essential information for tourists, ensuring a smooth and enjoyable entry into this tropical paradise.

Understanding Vanuatu's Visa Landscape: A Diversity of Entry Options

Vanuatu, a nation composed of 83 islands, embraces a diverse range of visitors, from those seeking short-term vacations to those contemplating longer stays. Understanding the visa landscape is the first step in planning a stress-free journey.

- Tourist Visa:

For most tourists, the tourist visa is the key to unlocking the beauty of Vanuatu. Many nationalities can obtain a visa on arrival, allowing for a hassle-free entry process. However, it's crucial to verify whether your country is eligible for this convenience or if you need to apply for a visa in advance.

- Business Visa:

If your visit involves business activities, such as meetings, conferences, or negotiations, a business visa may be more suitable. This type of visa accommodates the specific needs of individuals engaged in professional activities during their stay.

- Residence Visa:

For those with ambitions of a more prolonged stay or even making Vanuatu their temporary or permanent home, the residence visa is the pathway to explore. This visa involves a more extensive application process, often requiring additional documentation and approval from Vanuatu's immigration authorities.

Obtaining the Necessary Travel Permits: A Step-by-Step Guide

- Check Visa Requirements for Your Nationality:

Begin by researching the specific visa requirements for your nationality. The official government website of Vanuatu or the nearest embassy or consulate will provide accurate and up-to-date information. Be aware of any recent changes or updates to the visa policy.

- Determine the Appropriate Visa Type:

Identify the visa type that aligns with the purpose of your visit – whether it's tourism, business, or a more extended stay. This clarity streamlines the application process and ensures you meet all necessary criteria.

- Collect Required Documentation:

Compile the necessary documentation for your visa application. This may include a valid passport, proof of accommodation, return flight itinerary, financial statements, and any additional documents specified by Vanuatu's immigration authorities. Ensure your passport has sufficient validity beyond your intended departure date.

- Application Submission:

Submit your visa application through the designated channels, whether it's online, at a consulate or embassy, or upon arrival in Vanuatu. Accuracy is paramount, as any discrepancies could lead to delays or complications.

- Processing Time and Fees:

Understand the processing time for visa applications and any associated fees. Plan your trip accordingly to ensure that your travel documents are ready well before your departure date.

- Visa on Arrival:

If you are eligible for a visa on arrival, familiarize yourself with the process. Typically, this involves presenting your valid passport, proof of accommodation, and return flight details to immigration officials upon arrival at the airport in Vanuatu.

Special Entry Conditions: Navigating Unique Circumstances

- Health Requirements:

Stay informed about any health-related entry conditions, such as mandatory vaccinations or health screenings. Given the global health landscape, these requirements may change, so check for updates closer to your departure date.

- Customs and Import Regulations:

Familiarize yourself with Vanuatu's customs and import regulations to avoid any issues upon arrival. Certain items may be restricted or subject to customs duties, and adherence to these regulations is crucial for a smooth entry process.

- Respect Local Laws and Customs:

Understanding and respecting the local laws and customs of Vanuatu is essential. Familiarize yourself with cultural sensitivities and practices to ensure that your visit is not only enjoyable but also respectful to the local community.

1.4 Budgeting and Money Matters

Embarking on a journey to Vanuatu is not just an adventure of exploration but also a venture that requires thoughtful financial preparation. To make the most of your Vanuatu journey, it's essential to delve into the realm of budgeting and money management. This section provides valuable insights into creating a realistic travel budget, understanding the local currency, and maximizing your spending to ensure a financially smooth and enriching experience in this Pacific paradise.

1. Creating a Realistic Travel Budget:

Begin your financial preparation by crafting a detailed travel budget. Consider all aspects of your trip, including accommodation, meals, transportation, activities, and unforeseen expenses. Research average costs in Vanuatu to gauge realistic spending expectations. A well-thought-out budget not only helps you manage your finances effectively but also allows for a more relaxed and enjoyable experience without constant financial concerns.

2. Understanding Local Currency:

Vanuatu's official currency is the Vanuatu Vatu (VUV). Familiarize yourself with the current exchange rates and ensure that your budget is aligned with the local currency. While major credit cards are widely accepted in urban areas, having some local currency on hand is advisable, especially when venturing into more remote locations or local markets. ATMs are available in larger towns, providing convenient access to cash. Inform your bank about your travel dates to prevent any issues with using your cards abroad.

3. Tips for Maximizing Your Spending:

a. Explore Local Markets and Eateries: Vanuatu is home to vibrant local markets offering fresh produce, handmade crafts, and a glimpse into the daily life of the community. Explore these markets for cost-effective snacks, souvenirs, and a chance to engage with local culture.

b. Self-Catering Accommodations: Consider accommodations with kitchen facilities to prepare some of your meals. This not only provides a taste of local ingredients but also offers a budget-friendly alternative to dining out for every meal.

c. Utilize Public Transportation: Public transportation and shared shuttles are often more cost-effective than taxis.

Embrace the local experience by exploring the islands using these modes of transport.

d. Engage in Free or Low-Cost Activities: Vanuatu's natural beauty and cultural richness offer numerous activities that won't strain your budget. From pristine beaches and hiking trails to cultural sites, many attractions are either free or have minimal entrance fees.

e. Bargain at Markets: Local markets often allow for bargaining, so don't hesitate to negotiate for fair prices when purchasing souvenirs or locally crafted items.

4. Emergency Funds:

While meticulous planning is essential, it's equally important to set aside an emergency fund. Unforeseen circumstances such as medical emergencies or unexpected changes to your travel plans can arise. Having a contingency fund ensures that you're financially equipped to handle unexpected situations without jeopardizing the enjoyment of your trip.

5. Tipping and Service Charges:

Tipping is not customary in Vanuatu, but it is appreciated for exceptional service. Some restaurants may include a service charge, so it's advisable to check your bill before adding an additional tip. Understanding local customs regarding tipping ensures that you contribute appropriately to the local economy without unnecessary expenditures.

By incorporating these insights into your financial preparation, you can embark on your Vanuatu journey with confidence and financial resilience. From understanding the local currency to exploring budget-friendly activities, thoughtful money management enhances the overall travel experience, allowing you to immerse yourself fully in the wonders and culture of Vanuatu without unnecessary financial stress.

1.5 Essential Packing Tips

Packing for a journey to Vanuatu requires careful consideration to ensure you have everything you need for a comfortable and enjoyable stay in this tropical paradise. From practical essentials to specific items that enhance your experience, here are essential packing tips for tourists visiting Vanuatu:

1. Light and Breathable Clothing:

Pack lightweight and breathable clothing suitable for the tropical climate. Cotton and linen fabrics are ideal, providing comfort while allowing your skin to breathe. Consider including swimwear, shorts, T-shirts, and loose dresses for daytime   excursions.

2. Sun Protection:

Given Vanuatu's sun-drenched environment, sun protection is paramount. Pack sunscreen with high SPF, sunglasses, and a wide-brimmed hat to shield yourself from the strong Pacific sun. A reusable water bottle is also essential to stay hydrated throughout the day.

3. Insect Repellent:

Tropical destinations often come with insects, so packing a reliable insect repellent is crucial. Opt for a long-lasting formula to ward off mosquitoes and other insects, especially during outdoor activities or in the evenings.

4. Sturdy Footwear:

Bring comfortable and sturdy footwear suitable for various terrains. Sandals or flip-flops are ideal for the beach, while closed-toe shoes are advisable for hiking or exploring more rugged landscapes. Don't forget water shoes if you plan to engage in water activities.

5. Waterproof Gear:

Given Vanuatu's abundance of water-based activities, consider packing waterproof gear such as a dry bag to protect your belongings during island-hopping tours, snorkeling, or kayaking adventures.

6. Medications and First Aid Kit:

Pack any necessary prescription medications, along with a basic first aid kit. Include essentials like pain relievers, adhesive bandages, antiseptic wipes, and any specific medications you may require during your trip.

7. Electrical Adapters:

Vanuatu uses Type I electrical outlets, so ensure you bring the appropriate adapter for your electronic devices. This is crucial for keeping your devices charged and ready for capturing memorable moments.

8. Travel Documents:

Organize and secure your travel documents, including your passport, visa (if required), flight itineraries, accommodation reservations, and any travel insurance information. Consider carrying digital copies in case of emergencies.

9. Snorkeling Gear:

If snorkeling is on your itinerary, consider bringing your own snorkeling gear for a more personalized and hygienic experience. However, many tour operators also provide equipment if you prefer to travel light.

10. Lightweight Daypack:

- A compact daypack is handy for day trips, hikes, and beach outings. It allows you to carry essentials such as water, sunscreen, a camera, and a light jacket without being burdened by a large backpack.

11. Casual Evening Attire:

- While the dress code in Vanuatu is generally casual, packing a few slightly dressier options for evening outings or dinners at nicer restaurants is advisable. A light sweater or shawl may also come in handy for cooler evenings.

12. Bislama Phrasebook:

- While English and French are widely spoken, learning a few basic phrases in Bislama, the local language, can enhance your interactions and show respect for the local culture.

1.5.1 Travel-friendly luggage options

Choosing the right luggage for your Vanuatu adventure is a pivotal decision that can significantly impact the ease and enjoyment of your journey. From island hopping to exploring diverse landscapes, having travel-friendly luggage is essential. This section explores various luggage options, offering insights into what to consider when selecting the perfect travel companion for your Vanuatu getaway.

1. Backpacks and Daypacks:

For those planning to explore Vanuatu's natural wonders and engage in outdoor activities, a sturdy backpack is an excellent choice. Opt for a backpack with adjustable shoulder straps and multiple compartments for easy organization. A daypack is also essential for shorter excursions, providing a compact and convenient way to carry essentials such as water bottles, snacks, and cameras.

2. Wheeled Suitcases:

If your itinerary involves more urban exploration or you prefer the convenience of wheeled luggage, consider a durable suitcase with wheels. This type of luggage is ideal for navigating airports and well-paved areas. Choose a suitcase with a robust frame, quality wheels, and a handle that retracts fully to prevent any mishaps during your travels.

3. Duffel Bags:

Versatile and easy to stow away, duffel bags are a practical choice for travelers who need flexibility in their luggage. Look for a duffel with reinforced straps and durable material, ensuring it can withstand the rigors of travel. Some duffel bags also come with wheels for added convenience.

4. Waterproof or Water-Resistant Options:

Given Vanuatu's tropical climate and the possibility of unexpected rain, investing in waterproof or water-resistant luggage is a smart move. This helps protect your belongings from moisture and ensures that your essentials remain dry, especially if you're venturing near the beaches or engaging in water activities.

5. Lightweight and Compact Designs:

Keep in mind that you might need to maneuver your luggage through various modes of transportation, including boats and smaller aircraft for island hopping. Opt for lightweight and compact luggage options that are easy to carry and won't weigh you down during your travels.

6. Compression Bags:

For those looking to maximize space and keep clothing organized, compression bags are a game-changer. These bags allow you to compress your clothes, reducing the overall volume and making it easier to fit everything into your luggage. They are particularly useful for those who want to pack efficiently while still adhering to baggage weight restrictions.

7. Security Features:

Ensure that your chosen luggage provides adequate security features. Look for lockable zippers or built-in combination locks to secure your belongings. This is especially important if you plan to store your luggage in shared spaces or if you have valuable items that need extra protection.

8. Consider Local Transportation Conditions:

Given the diverse terrains in Vanuatu, consider the conditions of local transportation. If you anticipate navigating uneven surfaces or venturing off the beaten path, opt for luggage with sturdy wheels and a design that can handle rough terrain.

Final Tips:

- Check Airlines' Baggage Policies: Before finalizing your luggage choice, check the baggage policies of the airlines you'll be using. Ensure that your luggage meets size and weight requirements to avoid any unexpected fees.
- Packing Cubes: Consider using packing cubes to keep your belongings organized within your luggage, making it easier to locate items without unpacking everything.

CHAPTER TWO

GETTING ACQUAINTED WITH VANUATU

2.1 Overview of Vanuatu

Vanuatu, a captivating archipelago nestled in the heart of the South Pacific Ocean, stands as a testament to nature's grandeur and cultural diversity. Comprising 83 islands, each with its own distinct character, this paradisiacal nation beckons travelers with promises of pristine beaches, lush landscapes, and a tapestry of vibrant cultures. This section serves as a gateway to the wonders of Vanuatu, providing a comprehensive overview that encapsulates its geographical marvels, climate nuances, and the inimitable charm that makes it a coveted destination for explorers and adventure seekers alike.

Geographical Features:

Vanuatu's geography is nothing short of breathtaking. The archipelago stretches over 1,300 kilometers, encompassing 83 islands, and boasts an array of landscapes that range from volcanic terrains to dense rainforests. The islands are scattered across the South Pacific, forming a unique mosaic of ecosystems. From the towering peaks of Ambrym to the coral-fringed shores of Espiritu Santo, each island contributes to the visual symphony that defines Vanuatu.

The archipelago is renowned for its active volcanoes, and enthusiasts can witness nature's spectacular display on islands like Tanna. Mount Yasur, an iconic stratovolcano, invites intrepid travelers to witness its fiery eruptions, providing an awe-inspiring glimpse into the Earth's geological wonders.

Climate:

Vanuatu experiences a tropical climate that embodies the essence of paradise. The weather remains consistently warm throughout the year, with temperatures ranging from 23 to 30 degrees Celsius (73 to 86 degrees Fahrenheit). However, the archipelago is subject to seasonal variations, with a wet season from November to April and a dry season from May to October.

The tropical climate contributes to the lush greenery that blankets the islands, creating a haven for diverse flora and fauna. Visitors can revel in the enchanting beauty of tropical rainforests, explore vibrant coral reefs, and bask in the warm embrace of the South Pacific sun.

Unique Charm:

Vanuatu's allure extends beyond its natural beauty. The cultural tapestry woven by the indigenous people adds a unique charm to the visitor's experience. From traditional ceremonies that honor ancestral spirits to the rhythmic beats of custom dances, travelers have the opportunity to immerse themselves in the living traditions of the Ni-Vanuatu people.

The concept of 'island time' prevails, fostering a relaxed and unhurried atmosphere. This cultural trait invites visitors to embrace the unhurried pace of life, providing a refreshing contrast to the hustle and bustle of modern existence.

Whether exploring local markets, participating in customary celebrations, or simply enjoying a sunset on the beach, every moment in Vanuatu is an invitation to savor the beauty of the present.

2.2 Historical and Cultural Background

Delving into the rich tapestry of Vanuatu's history and culture is akin to embarking on a captivating journey through time, where the echoes of ancient traditions harmonize with the more recent imprints of colonial influences. This section peels back the layers of Vanuatu's cultural narrative, revealing a nation intricately woven by diverse forces that have shaped its identity.

Ancient Traditions:

Vanuatu's cultural heritage is deeply rooted in the traditions of its indigenous peoples, who have inhabited these islands for thousands of years. The Ni-Vanuatu people, with their strong connection to the land and sea, have fostered a lifestyle intricately intertwined with nature. Ancient practices, such as yam cultivation and intricate fishing techniques, not only sustained communities but also became integral elements of their cultural identity.

Customary systems, known as 'kastom,' play a pivotal role in the daily lives of the Ni-Vanuatu. These traditional practices encompass social structures, governance, and spiritual beliefs. The intricate kinship ties and communal living reflect a harmonious relationship with the environment and a commitment to preserving the cultural fabric that binds communities together.

Colonial Influences:

The arrival of European explorers and later, colonial powers, significantly impacted Vanuatu's cultural landscape. The archipelago witnessed a complex interplay of influences, as it became a focal point for European rivalry. Missionaries, traders, and later, colonial administrators left an indelible mark on the societal structures and cultural practices of the Ni-Vanuatu people.

The convergence of traditional beliefs with Christian teachings, for example, created a syncretic blend that is uniquely Ni-Vanuatu. The enduring resilience of indigenous customs amidst external pressures is a testament to the strength of Vanuatu's cultural identity.

Customary Practices and Ceremonial Rituals:

This section unfolds the vibrant tapestry of Vanuatu's cultural practices, which are deeply embedded in the fabric of everyday life. Customary ceremonies, with their elaborate dances, rhythmic chants, and symbolic rituals, offer a window into the spiritual dimensions of Ni-Vanuatu existence.

Ceremonies marking life events, such as birth, marriage, and death, are infused with cultural significance, illustrating the interconnectedness of individuals with their community and the spiritual realm. Traditional attire, body ornamentation, and the use of natural materials in these rituals underscore the importance of ancestral customs in shaping contemporary Ni-Vanuatu identity.

2.3 Languages and Communication

Embarking on a linguistic journey through Vanuatu reveals a captivating mosaic of over 110 indigenous languages, each a testament to the archipelago's rich cultural diversity. At the heart of this linguistic tapestry lies Bislama, a widely spoken Creole that unifies the islands and serves as a bridge among the varied linguistic communities. This section invites you to explore the significance of these languages, understand the role of Bislama in daily communication, and provides practical language tips to enrich your interactions with the warm and welcoming locals.

The Linguistic Diversity:

Vanuatu's linguistic diversity is unparalleled, with a multitude of languages spoken across its 83 islands. This diversity is a reflection of the distinct cultural groups that have flourished in isolation for centuries. Each language encapsulates the unique worldview, traditions, and stories of its respective community. While this diversity may seem overwhelming, it is a testament to the cultural richness that defines Vanuatu.

Bislama: The Common Thread:

In the midst of this linguistic tapestry, Bislama emerges as a unifying force. Born out of the necessity for communication between different language groups and European traders, Bislama is a Creole language that blends English, French, and indigenous languages. Its simplicity and adaptability have made it a lingua franca, facilitating communication among the Ni-Vanuatu people who may speak different native languages.

Significance of Traditional Languages:

While Bislama serves as a practical means of communication, traditional languages remain deeply significant. They are the vessels of cultural heritage, preserving ancient stories, rituals, and the unique identity of each community. The Ni-Vanuatu people take great pride in their linguistic heritage, viewing it as an integral part of their identity and a connection to their ancestors.

Role of Bislama in Daily Life:

Bislama transcends linguistic boundaries, becoming a language of everyday life in Vanuatu. From bustling marketplaces to tranquil village settings, Bislama is the medium through which people from different linguistic backgrounds interact. It is spoken in schools, government offices, and, most importantly, in the warm and lively conversations among friends and family.

Practical Language Tips:

Engaging with the locals in their language adds a layer of authenticity to your Vanuatu experience. While many Ni-Vanuatu people are multilingual and often speak Bislama, demonstrating an effort to use a few local phrases in their native language is met with genuine appreciation. Learning basic greetings, expressions of gratitude, and common phrases in Bislama can go a long way in fostering connections and breaking down cultural barriers.

When engaging in conversations, approach with a friendly demeanor, as the Ni-Vanuatu are known for their warmth and hospitality. Don't be shy about asking for language help;

locals are usually delighted to share their language and culture with visitors.

2.4 Currency and Exchange Tips

Vanuatu's official currency is the Vatu (VUV). The Vatu comes in both coins and banknotes, with denominations ranging from small change to larger bills. Familiarize yourself with the appearance and values of these denominations to facilitate smoother transactions during your stay.

Currency Exchange: Before You Go

- Pre-exchange Currency: Before arriving in Vanuatu, consider exchanging a small amount of your home currency for Vatu. This ensures that you have local cash on hand for immediate expenses upon arrival.
- Choose Reputable Services: Explore reliable currency exchange services, banks, or ATMs in your home country that offer competitive rates. It's advisable to check for any associated fees to make informed decisions.
- ATMs in Vanuatu: While major credit cards are widely accepted in urban areas, having local cash is essential, especially when venturing into more remote locations or local markets. ATMs are available in urban centers, providing convenient access to Vatu.

Navigating Transactions:

- Cash Transactions: In many local markets and smaller establishments, cash is the preferred method of payment. Ensure that you have a mix of smaller denominations, as some vendors may not have change for larger bills.

- Credit Cards: Major credit cards are accepted in hotels, restaurants, and larger businesses in urban areas. However, it's always a good idea to check in advance and have a backup payment method.

Tipping Customs:

- Tipping Practices: Tipping is not a widespread practice in Vanuatu, but it is appreciated in certain situations. Rounding up the bill or leaving a small amount as a gesture of appreciation is common, particularly in restaurants and cafes.
- Exceptional Service: If you receive exceptional service, consider expressing your gratitude through a modest tip. However, tipping is discretionary, and there is no strict expectation for it.

Financial Preparedness:

- Notify Your Bank: Inform your bank about your travel plans to Vanuatu to prevent any potential issues with credit or debit card transactions. This ensures that your financial transactions go smoothly during your stay.
- ATM Locations: Identify the locations of ATMs in the areas you plan to visit, especially if you are exploring outside major urban centers. Having this information beforehand can be helpful in managing your cash flow.

CHAPTER THREE

MUST VISIT DESTINATIONS

3.1 Port Vila Waterfront

As a tourist in Vanuatu, one of the most captivating destinations to include in your itinerary is the Port Vila Waterfront. Nestled on the shores of the South Pacific, Port Vila, the capital city of Vanuatu, offers a mesmerizing blend of natural beauty, cultural richness, and vibrant activities along its waterfront. In this comprehensive guide, we'll delve into the various facets of the Port Vila Waterfront, exploring its points of interest, cultural significance and recreational activities.

Overview of the Port Vila Waterfront

1. Location and Scenic Beauty:

Nestled along the enchanting coastline of Efate Island, the Port Vila Waterfront is a gem that beckons travelers with its strategic positioning and breathtaking vistas. Here, against the backdrop of the Pacific Ocean's azure waters, nature unveils its splendor. Pristine beaches stretch along the waterfront, inviting visitors to feel the soft, golden sands beneath their feet. Towering palm trees sway in the gentle breeze, casting a rhythmic dance of shadows on the ground. The vibrant coral reefs add a kaleidoscope of colors to the crystal-clear waters, creating a visual feast for tourists in search of a tropical paradise. Whether you're basking in the sun, enjoying a leisurely stroll, or capturing the sunset's hues, the Port Vila Waterfront's scenic beauty is an immersive experience that ctches Itself into the memories of every visitor.

2. Cultural Significance:

Beyond its natural allure, the Port Vila Waterfront holds profound cultural significance for the Ni-Vanuatu people. Serving as a dynamic hub for cultural expression, the waterfront becomes the stage for various events, ceremonies, and festivals that showcase the rich traditions of Vanuatu. Visitors are invited to partake in these cultural celebrations, gaining insights into age-old customs and rituals that define the identity of the Ni-Vanuatu. From traditional dances to spiritual ceremonies, the Port Vila Waterfront becomes a living canvas where the vibrant tapestry of Vanuatu's cultural heritage is on display. This intersection of natural beauty and cultural richness transforms a visit to the Port Vila Waterfront into a holistic and immersive journey, offering travelers not just scenic delights but also a deep connection with the heart and soul of Vanuatu.

Points of Interest

1. Havannah Street Market:

As you explore the Port Vila Waterfront, a captivating cultural immersion awaits at the Havannah Street Market, positioned in proximity to the waterfront's vibrant edge. This bustling market serves as a portal to the heart of local life, where visitors can partake in the daily rhythm of Vanuatu's community spirit. Traverse the market's lanes adorned with an eclectic array of stalls, showcasing not only the freshest produce from the land and sea but also an assortment of local crafts and traditional artifacts. Engage in conversations with the friendly locals, who are more than willing to share stories about their culture and way of life. Indulge your senses by sampling exotic fruits, their flavors heightened by the tropical sun, and allow the vibrant colors of the market to seep into your memories. Before bidding farewell, consider acquiring unique souvenirs—a handmade artifact or a piece of local craftsmanship—to serve as tangible memories of your immersive visit to Havannah Street Market.

2. Port Vila Markets:

Situated in close proximity to the Port Vila Waterfront, the Port Vila Markets beckon with a lively atmosphere that encapsulates the essence of daily life in Vanuatu. The markets stand as a testament to the island nation's rich agricultural and artisanal heritage. Here, amidst the bustling stalls, locals gather to trade a diverse array of goods, creating a vibrant tapestry of color and culture. Traverse the market's lively alleys, where the aroma of fresh fruits and vegetables mingles with the scent of aromatic spices. Marvel at the intricate craftsmanship of handmade souvenirs and traditional artifacts that reflect the skill and artistry of Vanuatu's artisans. The Port Vila Markets provide an authentic and dynamic glimpse into the pulse of daily existence on the islands, making it an ideal destination for those seeking an immersive and culturally enriching experience during their visit to the Port Vila Waterfront.

3. Memorials and Monuments:

Along the Port Vila Waterfront, poignant memorials and monuments stand as silent tributes to Vanuatu's rich history. The War Memorial, a solemn structure, honors the nation's sacrifices during World War II, serving as a reminder of the resilience and courage of the Ni-Vanuatu people. Additionally, other monuments celebrate milestones such as independence and cultural achievements, creating a historical narrative that unfolds against the backdrop of the Pacific Ocean.

4. Seafront Restaurants and Cafés:

Elevate your culinary experience at the Port Vila Waterfront by indulging in the offerings of its seafront restaurants and cafés. These establishments, with their charming ambiance, not only provide a delectable array of local delicacies, fresh seafood, and international cuisine but also offer panoramic views of the ocean. Sunset dining transforms the seafront into a romantic haven, where the warm hues of the descending sun create an enchanting backdrop for an unforgettable dining experience. Whether savoring local flavors or international delights, the seafront eateries invite you to relish not just the cuisine but also the captivating beauty that surrounds you.

5. Waterfront Parks:

Discover tranquility as you meander through the lush and meticulously landscaped waterfront parks, exemplified by the enchanting Seafront Park. Here, amidst tropical gardens, you can unwind and revel in the gentle coastal breeze. Seafront Park, along with other captivating green spaces along the Port Vila Waterfront, provides an idyllic setting for relaxation. Moreover, these parks often serve as vibrant venues for cultural events, captivating live performances, and spirited local celebrations. Whether you seek a peaceful retreat surrounded by nature or wish to immerse yourself in the dynamic cultural pulse of Vanuatu, the waterfront parks offer a harmonious blend of both, ensuring a delightful and refreshing experience for every visitor.

Recreational Activities

1. Water Sports:

Embrace your adventurous spirit at the Port Vila Waterfront, where a plethora of exhilarating water sports awaits. Dive into the crystal-clear waters and partake in activities like snorkeling, allowing you to witness the mesmerizing dance of vibrant marine life amid stunning coral reefs. Kayaking offers a more leisurely exploration, allowing you to paddle along the coastline and soak in the breathtaking views of the Pacific Ocean. For those seeking a balance challenge, stand-up paddleboarding is a popular choice, providing a unique perspective of the waterfront's beauty. Whether you're a novice or an experienced water enthusiast, the Port Vila Waterfront caters to all, inviting you to immerse yourself in the wonders beneath the surface and create lasting memories of aquatic adventures.

2. Boat Tours and Cruises:

Embark on a maritime exploration of Vanuatu's coastal wonders with boat tours and cruises departing from the Port Vila Waterfront. These excursions unveil the beauty of surrounding islands and hidden coves, transporting you to pristine landscapes only accessible by water. Whether you opt for a day trip to nearby islets or a romantic sunset cruise, these boat tours offer a unique perspective of Vanuatu's coastal beauty. Revel in the scenic splendor, witness the play of sunlight on the waves, and create memories against the backdrop of the South Pacific's enchanting horizons. The Port Vila Waterfront becomes your gateway to maritime adventures, promising an immersive experience that perfectly complements the natural allure of this Pacific paradise.

3. Diving Adventures:

For diving enthusiasts, the Port Vila Waterfront unveils a world beneath the waves, offering an exceptional gateway to underwater wonders. Explore renowned dive sites that adorn the coastal expanse, from intricate coral gardens to mysterious submerged caves. The crystal-clear waters provide a window to a vibrant marine ecosystem, teeming with a kaleidoscope of colors and diverse marine life. Immerse yourself in the underwater ballet of tropical fish, graceful rays, and intricate coral formations. Whether you're a seasoned diver or a beginner, the Port Vila Waterfront caters to all levels of expertise, promising unforgettable diving adventures against the backdrop of Vanuatu's coastal beauty.

4. Cultural Performances:

Enrich your Vanuatu experience by immersing yourself in the cultural tapestry that unfolds along the Port Vila Waterfront. Attend live performances that showcase the richness of Vanuatu's cultural heritage. The seafront stages come alive with traditional dances, rhythmic music, and captivating rituals that have been passed down through generations. Engage with the performers and absorb the authentic spirit of Ni-Vanuatu traditions. These cultural performances, often accompanied by vibrant costumes and storytelling, offer visitors a profound insight into the customs and beliefs that define Vanuatu's unique identity. Whether it's an impromptu gathering or a scheduled event, the waterfront becomes a dynamic platform for cultural immersion, allowing you to connect with the heart and soul of this Pacific island nation.

5. Fishing Excursions:

Experience the essence of the South Pacific by embarking on a fishing excursion departing from the Port Vila Waterfront. The waters surrounding Vanuatu are a haven for game fish, and fishing enthusiasts have the opportunity to reel in prized catches such as marlin and tuna. Joining a fishing expedition offers not only the thrill of the chase but also a chance to appreciate the maritime beauty of the region. The expert guides provide insights into the local fishing culture and ensure a memorable outing for anglers of all levels. Whether you are seeking a leisurely fishing experience or an adrenaline-pumping adventure, the fishing excursions from the waterfront promise an authentic taste of Vanuatu's seafaring traditions against the backdrop of the open ocean.

3.2 Mele Cascades

When exploring the tropical paradise of Vanuatu, one cannot miss the enchanting beauty of Mele Cascades, a natural wonder nestled amidst lush rainforest landscapes. This cascading waterfall, located just a short drive from Port Vila, offers visitors a serene escape into nature's embrace. From its pristine pools to the vibrant flora surrounding the area, Mele Cascades stands as a must-visit destination for tourists seeking both relaxation and adventure.

1. Introduction to Mele Cascades

- Location and Accessibility

Mele Cascades is situated approximately 10 kilometers northeast of Port Vila, the capital city of Vanuatu. The ease of access makes it a popular choice for day trips or half-day excursions, attracting tourists looking to experience the natural beauty that defines this South Pacific archipelago.

- Natural Beauty and Tranquility

The cascading waterfalls, formed by the Mele River as it makes its way down the lush hills of Efate Island, create a picturesque scene that captivates the senses. The crystal-clear water, surrounded by vibrant greenery, provides a tranquil atmosphere, inviting visitors to unwind and connect with the pristine environment.

2. A Closer Look: Features of Mele Cascades

- Multi-Tiered Waterfalls: A Symphony of Nature's Elegance

Mele Cascades unveils a natural spectacle with its series of multi-tiered waterfalls, each presenting a distinct and mesmerizing panorama. The cascading water gracefully descends over ancient volcanic rock formations, creating a visual symphony that captivates every observer. As the water journeys downward, it forms inviting pools at various levels, crafting a natural staircase effect that enhances the allure of this South Pacific gem.

- Refreshing Pools: Nature's Oasis for Relaxation and Adventure

The pools at Mele Cascades are not only visually captivating but also serve as nature's refreshing oasis. The cool, clear waters beckon visitors to take a rejuvenating dip, surrounded by the ambient sounds of nature. These pools provide an exceptional opportunity for both relaxation and adventure, catering to those seeking a tranquil escape as well as thrill-seekers ready to embrace the excitement. For the daring at heart, cliff-jumping into the deeper sections of the pools adds an extra dimension to the experience, creating lasting memories amid the pristine beauty of Vanuatu.

- Surrounding Flora and Fauna: A Rainforest Journey of Discovery

The journey to Mele Cascades is an immersive experience in itself, leading visitors through a lush and vibrant rainforest. The trail to the waterfall unveils the diverse flora and fauna that define the ecological richness of Vanuatu. Towering trees with canopies that seem to touch the sky, an array of vibrant flowers painting the forest floor, and the melodic songs of native birds create a sensory-rich tapestry. As you traverse the trail, the rainforest becomes a living testament to the untouched beauty of the island, inviting you to connect with nature on a profound level. Mele Cascades not only captivates with its waterfalls and pools but also with the surrounding ecological wonders that make every step toward the destination an integral part of the overall enchantment.

3. Exploring Mele Cascades: Practical Tips

- Guided Tours

To make the most of your visit, consider joining a guided tour to Mele Cascades. Knowledgeable local guides provide insights into the ecological significance of the area, share cultural anecdotes, and ensure your safety during the trek. Guided tours also enhance the overall experience by offering a deeper understanding of the surroundings.

- Trail Difficulty and Duration

The trek to Mele Cascades is a moderate hike suitable for visitors of various fitness levels. The well-maintained trail is equipped with stairs and handrails, making it accessible to a wide range of travelers. The duration of the hike is approximately 15-20 minutes, ensuring that you can enjoy the natural beauty without an overly strenuous journey.

What to Bring

- Swimwear: Don't forget to bring your swimwear to take advantage of the inviting pools at the base of the waterfall.
- Comfortable Footwear: Wear comfortable walking shoes suitable for a nature hike.
- Sun Protection: Apply sunscreen and wear a hat to protect yourself from the sun.
- Water and Snacks: Stay hydrated by bringing a water bottle, and pack some snacks to enjoy amidst the natural surroundings.

- Camera: Capture the breathtaking moments and scenery with a camera or smartphone.

Respect for the Environment

While exploring Mele Cascades, it's essential to practice responsible tourism. Respect the natural environment by sticking to designated trails, avoiding littering, and refraining from disturbing the local flora and fauna. Following sustainable tourism practices ensures that this pristine destination remains unspoiled for future generations.

4. Cultural Significance of Mele Cascades

- Ni-Vanuatu Legends: Echoes of Cultural Heritage

Mele Cascades transcends its natural beauty, holding profound cultural significance for the Ni-Vanuatu people. Within the cascading waters and ancient rocks lies a tapestry of legends, passed down through generations. These stories not only enrich the experience of Mele Cascades but also serve as a testament to the deep connection between the Ni-Vanuatu people and the natural elements that surround them. These legends, woven with reverence and tradition, add a layer of cultural richness, inviting visitors to delve into the narratives that have shaped the cultural identity of Vanuatu.

- Rituals and Ceremonies: Celebrating Cultural Heritage

Mele Cascades serves as more than a picturesque destination; it is a sacred setting where the lushness and cascading waters become the backdrop for traditional rituals and ceremonies. The Ni-Vanuatu people, deeply connected to their cultural heritage, come together in this natural sanctuary to celebrate and honor their traditions. Visitors fortunate enough to be present during these moments may witness or even participate in these authentic cultural experiences, forging a deeper connection with the living heritage of Vanuatu. Mele Cascades, therefore, becomes not only a feast for the eyes but also a portal into the cultural soul of the Ni-Vanuatu people, where past and present intertwine in a celebration of identity and tradition.

5. Practicalities: Getting There and Entrance Fees

- Transportation

Mele Cascades is easily accessible from Port Vila. Visitors can hire a taxi, join an organized tour, or rent a car for a short drive to the site. The scenic journey itself offers glimpses of Vanuatu's landscapes, preparing you for the natural beauty that awaits.

- Entrance Fees

There is an entrance fee to access Mele Cascades, and it's advisable to check the current rates before planning your visit. The fees often contribute to the maintenance and preservation of the site, ensuring its sustainability as a tourist attraction.

3.3 Mount Yasur

Mount Yasur stands as a majestic testament to the raw power and beauty of nature. An active stratovolcano on

Tanna Island, Mount Yasur beckons adventurers and nature enthusiasts alike. This comprehensive guide is designed to provide tourists visiting Vanuatu with all the necessary information to make the most of their experience at Mount Yasur, from its geological marvels to practical tips for a safe and immersive journey.

1. Understanding Mount Yasur: Nature's Fiery Spectacle

- Geological Significance

Mount Yasur stands as a geological marvel, distinguished globally as one of the most accessible and consistently active volcanoes. Visitors are granted a front-row seat to the enthralling spectacle of molten lava dancing within the volcano's crater. Its significance lies in being a stratovolcano, characterized by its steep conical shape formed through the accumulation of alternating layers of solidified lava, volcanic ash, and rocks. Grasping the intricacies of Mount Yasur's structure not only enriches the visitor's experience but also deepens the understanding of the dynamic geological forces that shape our planet beneath the Earth's surface.

- Cultural Significance

Beyond its geological allure, Mount Yasur holds profound cultural and spiritual importance for the indigenous Ni-Vanuatu people. Revered as a sacred site, this stratovolcano is enveloped in local customs dictating specific protocols for visitors. Respecting these cultural sensitivities becomes paramount, adding a layer of reverence to the overall experience and fostering a harmonious interaction between tourists and the indigenous community. Acknowledging the cultural significance of Mount Yasur enhances the journey, allowing visitors to engage with the natural wonder while honoring the spiritual heritage of the land.

2. Planning Your Visit to Mount Yasur

- Best Time to Visit

While the allure of Mount Yasur beckons year-round, the optimal time for an unforgettable visit is during the dry season from May to October. This period ensures a clearer and more unobstructed view of the volcanic activity, as the skies are generally free from the haze that may obscure visibility. Choosing to embark on this adventure during the dry season enhances the chances of witnessing the breathtaking eruptions and the mesmerizing display of molten lava against the night sky.

- Guided Tours and Safety Measures

Embarking on a guided tour is not only a recommended choice but also a gateway to a safer and more enriching experience at Mount Yasur. Local guides, with their intimate knowledge of the terrain, provide valuable insights into the volcano's behavior, geological features, and cultural significance. Opt for tour operators that prioritize safety, ensuring that they adhere to strict safety protocols and provide essential equipment such as gas masks. This ensures that visitors can marvel at the volcanic wonders with peace of mind, guided by experts who understand the nuances of this dynamic natural phenomenon.

- Physical Preparation

Ascending to the summit of Mount Yasur involves a moderate hike, underscoring the importance of physical preparation for visitors. Enhance your overall experience by donning comfortable hiking shoes, suitable clothing, and staying adequately hydrated throughout the trek. Preparedness ensures that the journey to witness Mount Yasur's fiery spectacle is not only enjoyable but also allows for a deeper connection with the natural beauty of the volcano and its surroundings.

3. Reaching Mount Yasur: The Journey to Tanna Island

- Transportation

Embarking on the journey to witness Mount Yasur's awe-inspiring volcanic activity typically begins with a flight from Vanuatu's capital, Port Vila, to White Grass Airport on Tanna Island. With airlines operating regular flights, this leg of the journey is relatively convenient for tourists. Once you land on Tanna, the next step is reaching the base of the volcano. Guided tours, known for their expertise in navigating the island's terrain, or local transportation options are available to seamlessly transport you to the foothills of Mount Yasur. This leg of the adventure offers glimpses of Tanna's scenic landscapes, setting the stage for the volcanic spectacle that awaits.

- Accommodations on Tanna Island

Tanna Island offers a range of accommodations, ensuring that visitors can find a comfortable retreat after a day of exploration. From eco-friendly resorts nestled in lush surroundings to cozy guesthouses, the island caters to various preferences and budgets. To secure your preferred lodging, especially during peak tourist seasons, it is advisable to book accommodations in advance. This ensures not only a hassle-free stay but also the opportunity to unwind in the tranquility of Tanna's natural beauty, providing a perfect complement to the exhilarating experience of witnessing Mount Yasur's volcanic wonders.

4. Experiencing Mount Yasur: A Journey into the Volcanic Wonderland

- Sunset Spectacle

The magic of Mount Yasur extends to the twilight hours, making a sunset visit an integral part of the experience. As the sun dips below the horizon, the changing hues of the sky create a mesmerizing backdrop to the volcanic eruptions. Guided tours often structure their itineraries to include this enchanting moment, allowing visitors to witness the transition from daylight to the captivating night spectacle. The volcanic activity against the backdrop of the setting sun casts an otherworldly glow over the landscape, transforming the surroundings into a canvas of vivid colors.

- Nighttime Views

As darkness envelops Mount Yasur, the volcanic wonders take center stage with an intensified fiery glow. The molten lava, propelled into the night sky, becomes even more pronounced, creating a surreal ambiance. The contrast between the luminescent lava and the dark expanse of the night sky offers a unique and awe-inspiring perspective on the raw power and beauty of Mount Yasur. Observing the volcanic activity under the cover of night adds an extra layer of drama and mystique, turning the entire experience into a once-in-a-lifetime journey into the heart of Vanuatu's natural wonders.

4.3 Volcanic Eruptions

The hallmark of Mount Yasur's captivating allure lies in its renowned strombolian-style eruptions, setting it apart as one of the world's most remarkable volcanic phenomena. Characterized by frequent and moderate explosions, these eruptions propel glowing lava into the air, painting the night sky with a breathtaking display of natural pyrotechnics. The rhythmic explosions create an awe-inspiring spectacle, each burst contributing to the mesmerizing dance of molten lava against the backdrop of Tanna's darkness. This continuous display of volcanic activity is a hallmark of Mount Yasur, offering observers a front-row seat to the dynamic forces that shape our planet. It's a once-in-a-lifetime experience that beckons travelers from around the globe, drawing them to the heart of Vanuatu for an encounter with the raw, elemental power and beauty of this extraordinary natural wonder.

5. Responsible Tourism at Mount Yasur

- Environmental Considerations

While visiting Mount Yasur, it is crucial to practice responsible tourism. Adhering to designated paths and respecting the natural surroundings helps minimize the ecological impact on the volcano and its ecosystem. Avoid littering, and follow the guidance of local guides to ensure a sustainable experience.

- Cultural Respect

Respecting the cultural significance of Mount Yasur to the Ni-Vanuatu people is paramount. Visitors are encouraged to adhere to local customs, such as seeking permission before capturing photographs and refraining from engaging in disruptive behavior. Building positive relationships with the local community contributes to the preservation of this sacred site.

3.4 Champagne Beach, Espiritu Santo

Nestled on the northern shores of Espiritu Santo, the largest island in the Vanuatu archipelago, Champagne Beach stands as an exquisite testament to nature's artistry. Renowned for its crystal-clear turquoise waters, powdery white sands, and a unique underwater phenomenon that mimics effervescent champagne, this pristine stretch of coastline is a must-visit destination for travelers seeking tranquility, natural beauty, and a touch of wonder.

1. Introduction to Champagne Beach

- Location and Accessibility

Champagne Beach is situated approximately 30 kilometers to the east of Luganville, the largest town on Espiritu Santo. Accessible by road, this tropical haven is a scenic drive through lush landscapes and charming villages. The journey to Champagne Beach itself is an adventure, offering glimpses of the island's diverse flora and fauna.

- The Enchanting Waters of Champagne Beach

The beach owes its name to the effervescent bubbles that naturally rise from the sea floor, creating a delightful sensation akin to sipping champagne. This natural wonder occurs due to an underground freshwater spring that releases carbon dioxide, creating a mesmerizing display of bubbles in the shallow waters. The contrast between the effervescent bubbles and the serene, crystal-clear sea makes Champagne Beach a unique and captivating destination.

2. Planning Your Visit

- Best Time to Visit

Champagne Beach is a year-round destination, but the dry season from May to October is considered the ideal time to visit. During these months, the weather is typically sunny and dry, providing perfect conditions for enjoying the beach and its surroundings.

Entry Requirements

As with any travel destination, it's essential to check the entry requirements for Vanuatu, including visa regulations and any specific guidelines related to the ongoing global situation. Ensure that your travel documents are in order for a smooth entry into this tropical paradise.

3. Experiencing Champagne Beach: A Comprehensive Guide

- Scenic Beauty and Relaxation

As visitors step onto Champagne Beach, they are immediately enveloped in a scene reminiscent of a tropical paradise postcard. The soft, powdery sand unfolds beneath towering palm trees, creating an inviting canvas for beachgoers to unwind. Whether seeking shade under the palms or basking in the warm tropical sun, the atmosphere exudes tranquility. The calm, inviting waters further enhance the experience, providing an idyllic setting for a leisurely swim or a revitalizing snorkeling adventure.

- Underwater Delights: Snorkeling and Diving

For enthusiasts of underwater exploration, Champagne Beach is a gateway to a mesmerizing marine world. The clear waters that embrace the shore boast vibrant coral reefs teeming with a kaleidoscope of colorful fish. Dive enthusiasts and snorkelers alike will be enchanted by the abundance of marine life just beneath the surface. Conveniently, snorkeling equipment is readily available for rent, allowing visitors to immerse themselves in the captivating underwater realm surrounding Champagne Beach.

- Picnicking and Beachside Activities

Beyond its natural beauty, Champagne Beach offers more than just sun and sea – it provides an ideal setting for a leisurely beachside picnic. Whether visitors bring their own supplies or explore nearby vendors offering delicious local snacks, the beach's tranquil ambiance creates the perfect backdrop for creating lasting memories. Enjoying a meal on the shores of Champagne Beach is a delightful experience, allowing travelers to savor the breathtaking natural scenery while creating a connection with this pristine coastal haven.

4. Respecting Nature and Culture

- Environmental Conservation

Champagne Beach is a pristine natural environment, and visitors are encouraged to practice responsible tourism. Be mindful of the surroundings, avoid leaving any waste behind, and follow designated paths to minimize impact on the delicate ecosystems.

5. Logistical Considerations

- Accommodations

While Champagne Beach itself beckons as a day-trip destination, travelers have a range of accommodation options awaiting them in the charming town of Luganville. From budget-friendly guesthouses that provide a cozy retreat to more luxurious resorts offering a touch of indulgence, Luganville caters to diverse preferences. Opting to stay in Luganville not only ensures easy access to the pristine shores of Champagne Beach but also serves as a comfortable and well-equipped base for exploring the myriad attractions scattered across Espiritu Santo.

- Transportation

Embarking on the journey to Champagne Beach is an integral part of the adventure, and visitors have various transportation options to choose from. Those seeking convenience can hire local transportation services, while those with an adventurous spirit may opt to rent a vehicle, allowing them to relish the scenic drive from Luganville to the beach. For a more immersive experience, guided tours are readily available, offering not only transportation but also valuable insights into the local culture and geography, enriching the journey to this tropical oasis on Espiritu Santo

6. Exploring Beyond Champagne Beach

- Blue Holes of Espiritu Santo

Beyond the enchanting allure of Champagne Beach, Espiritu Santo unveils a realm of natural wonders, and among the must-visit destinations are the renowned Blue Holes. As a traveler, it's highly recommended not to miss the opportunity to explore these captivating natural phenomena, with notable mentions including the Nanda Blue Hole and the Matevulu Blue Hole.

Immerse yourself in the surreal beauty of the Nanda Blue Hole, where the crystal-clear freshwater pool is framed by lush vegetation, creating an oasis of tranquility. The vibrant hues of blue, ranging from azure to turquoise, are a visual feast, and the clarity of the water invites visitors to take a refreshing plunge into its cool embrace.

Equally mesmerizing is the Matevulu Blue Hole, another jewel in Espiritu Santo's natural crown. Surrounded by dense tropical foliage, this freshwater pool is a haven for those seeking serenity and a break from the tropical heat. The brilliance of the blue water, combined with the natural ambiance, creates an atmosphere of unparalleled beauty, making it a perfect spot for relaxation and rejuvenation.

Both the Nanda and Matevulu Blue Holes exemplify the pristine and untouched beauty of Espiritu Santo. Exploring these freshwater pools not only provides a visual spectacle but also offers a unique opportunity to connect with nature in a way that is both surreal and deeply refreshing. The Blue Holes stand as testaments to the island's extraordinary natural diversity, inviting visitors to venture beyond the shoreline and discover the hidden gems that make Espiritu Santo a truly magical destination.

3.5 Million Dollar Point

Among the many hidden gems waiting to be discovered by intrepid travelers, "Million Dollar Point" stands out as a remarkable attraction with a fascinating history and an underwater spectacle that captivates the imagination. In this comprehensive guide, we delve into the depths of Million Dollar Point, uncovering its historical significance, the vibrant marine life that surrounds it, and practical tips for tourists eager to explore this extraordinary site.

1. A Glimpse into History

- The Legacy of World War II

Million Dollar Point stands as a poignant testament to Vanuatu's role in the closing chapters of World War II. In those tumultuous times, the United States strategically stationed troops and established military bases in Vanuatu, then referred to as the New Hebrides. As the war neared its end, the U.S. military grappled with the colossal task of repatriating an immense quantity of equipment and supplies from these Pacific islands.

- The Decision to Dump Equipment

Faced with the logistical challenge of transporting surplus military gear back to the United States, a pivotal decision was made to dispose of the equipment in the waters near Luganville on Espiritu Santo, the largest island in Vanuatu. This decision gave rise to what we now know as Million Dollar Point—an underwater treasure trove holding a diverse array of military artifacts, ranging from trucks and jeeps to bulldozers and various other war materiel.

- The Million Dollar Point Name

The evocative name "Million Dollar Point" finds its roots in the estimated value of the abandoned military equipment. This decision to deliberately sink rather than recover the equipment was not merely a pragmatic solution to a logistical challenge; it also carried strategic significance. By scuttling the surplus military supplies in this manner, the U.S. military ensured that valuable resources did not fall into the hands of potential adversaries, adding a layer of historical intrigue to the underwater legacy of Million Dollar Point.

2. Diving into the Depths

- The Underwater Spectacle

Million Dollar Point beckons diving enthusiasts to explore its extraordinary underwater spectacle, establishing itself as a must-visit destination. As you descend into the azure depths, a surreal landscape unfolds before you—military artifacts adorned in colorful coral create an otherworldly scene, surrounded by the gentle dance of marine life. The sunken machinery has evolved into artificial reefs, transforming the ocean floor into a hauntingly beautiful setting that captivates divers with its unique allure.

- Marine Life Abounds

The submerged world of Million Dollar Point is not only a historical repository but also a thriving ecosystem. Flourishing marine life adds vibrancy to the site, attracting a diverse array of underwater inhabitants. Schools of tropical fish gracefully weave through the submerged vehicles, and vibrant coral formations have taken root on the surfaces of the military equipment. This abundance of marine life adds an extra layer of enchantment to the historical significance of Million Dollar Point, creating an immersive experience that seamlessly combines the past with the vibrant present of the underwater world.

3. Planning Your Visit

- Location and Accessibility

Million Dollar Point is conveniently located near Luganville on the island of Espiritu Santo. Luganville is the second-largest town in Vanuatu and serves as the primary gateway for accessing this historical site. Travelers can reach Espiritu Santo via domestic flights from Port Vila, the capital of Vanuatu.

- Diving Requirements and Operators

Diving at Million Dollar Point requires a sense of adventure and a basic level of scuba diving proficiency. Numerous dive operators in Luganville offer guided tours to this underwater treasure. It's advisable to check the availability of guided dives, equipment rental options, and any certification requirements before planning your visit.

- Best Time to Visit

Vanuatu's climate is generally warm and tropical throughout the year, making Million Dollar Point accessible for diving almost any time. However, the dry season, from May to October, is considered the best time to visit when the weather conditions are optimal for diving, and the visibility underwater is at its peak.

- Accommodations in Luganville

Luganville offers a range of accommodations catering to various budgets and preferences. From boutique resorts to budget-friendly guesthouses, tourists can find a comfortable place to stay while exploring the attractions of Espiritu Santo, including Million Dollar Point.

4. Respecting the Site and Safety Considerations

- Responsible Diving Practices

While exploring the underwater wonders of Million Dollar Point, it's crucial for divers to adhere to responsible and sustainable practices. Avoid touching or disturbing the marine life and artifacts, as this helps preserve the delicate balance of the ecosystem. Responsible diving ensures that future generations can continue to appreciate the historical and natural beauty of the site.

- Safety Precautions

Before embarking on a diving expedition to Million Dollar Point, it's essential to prioritize safety. Confirm that your scuba diving equipment is in proper working condition, and ensure that you are adequately trained for underwater exploration. Following safety guidelines provided by dive operators is crucial for an enjoyable and secure experience.

3.6 Hideaway Island

Hideaway Island, situated just off the coast of the main island of Efate, is a captivating retreat renowned for its crystal-clear waters, vibrant marine life, and the allure of being one of the world's first marine sanctuaries. This small coral island is accessible via a short boat ride from the mainland, making it an easily reachable sanctuary for those seeking an escape from the hustle and bustle of everyday life.

Getting There:

- From Port Vila:

Most travelers will embark on their journey to Hideaway Island from Port Vila, the capital of Vanuatu. Boats regularly depart from the Emten Lagoon, providing a picturesque journey to the island. The boat ride itself is an adventure, offering glimpses of the vibrant marine life beneath the surface.

- Boat Transfers:

Resorts and tour operators often arrange boat transfers for guests, ensuring a seamless journey to Hideaway Island. It's advisable to confirm the availability of transfers in advance to make the most of your visit.

Accommodations:

- Hideaway Haven

While Hideaway Island is renowned for its day-trip allure, some visitors may choose to extend their stay and revel in the tranquility of this secluded paradise. The island boasts eco-friendly accommodations, ranging from beachfront bungalows to cozy cottages, allowing guests to wake up to the soothing sounds of the ocean and the breathtaking views of the surrounding coral reefs.

Underwater Post Office:

- Dive into a Unique Experience

One of the most distinctive features of Hideaway Island is its underwater post office, recognized by the Guinness World Records as the world's only underwater post office. Snorkel or dive to the ocean floor and send a postcard from this unique postal service, complete with the island's special postmark. It's a novel experience that combines adventure with the age-old tradition of sending letters.

Marine Sanctuary and Snorkeling:

- Coral Gardens:

As you venture into the underwater realm surrounding Hideaway Island, the coral gardens unfold as a mesmerizing spectacle. This marine sanctuary serves as a haven for a rich diversity of marine life, offering snorkelers a front-row seat to the vibrant underwater tapestry. Dive into the crystal-clear waters and witness the kaleidoscope of colors as schools of fish dance among the intricate coral formations. The coral gardens are a testament to the pristine ecosystem that thrives beneath the surface, providing an immersive encounter with the natural wonders of the South Pacific.

- Giant Clam Nursery:

Embark on a journey to the giant clam nursery, a truly enchanting destination near Hideaway Island. Here, you'll witness these magnificent creatures in their natural habitat, revealing an array of iridescent colors that captivate the imagination. Beyond being a visual delight, the nursery stands as a testament to ongoing conservation efforts dedicated to preserving the marine ecosystem. This encounter not only offers a glimpse into the grandeur of these underwater giants but also underscores the importance of safeguarding the delicate balance of marine life.

- Guided Snorkeling Tours:

For an in-depth exploration of Hideaway Island's underwater wonders, take advantage of guided snorkeling tours. Tailored for both beginners and experienced enthusiasts, these tours provide an opportunity to navigate the marine sanctuary with the expertise of local guides. Discover hidden corners, encounter unique marine species, and gain insights into the delicate biodiversity flourishing beneath the ocean's surface. Guided by knowledgeable locals, these tours transform your snorkeling experience into an educational and awe-inspiring journey through the heart of Vanuatu's aquatic paradise.

Diving Adventures:

- PADI Dive Center:

Dive enthusiasts at Hideaway Island can elevate their underwater exploration through the PADI Dive Center. Whether you're a novice or an experienced diver, this center caters to all skill levels, offering a spectrum of courses and guided dives to explore the captivating dive sites nearby. Immerse yourself in the underwater wonders, from intricate underwater caves to mesmerizing coral-covered walls. The PADI Dive Center ensures a safe and exhilarating experience, providing divers with the tools to unlock the mysteries of Vanuatu's aquatic realm.

- Night Dives:

For those with an adventurous spirit, Hideaway Island presents the opportunity for night dives, offering a unique perspective of the underwater world. As daylight gives way to darkness, witness the emergence of nocturnal marine life, including mesmerizing bioluminescent creatures. This ethereal experience adds a surreal touch to your diving adventures, unveiling the magic that unfolds beneath the surface when the sun sets on Hideaway Island.

Beach Activities and Relaxation:

- White Sandy Beaches:

While Hideaway Island is a haven for aquatic enthusiasts, its shores are adorned with pristine white sandy beaches that invite visitors to unwind and soak up the tropical sun. The gentle lapping of the waves against the shore creates a soothing ambiance, providing the perfect backdrop for relaxation.

- Hammocks and Coconut Trees:

Numerous hammocks strung between coconut trees offer the ideal spot to laze away the day, providing a front-row seat to the mesmerizing views of the Pacific. Whether you're engrossed in a good book or simply savoring the tranquility, the island's natural beauty enhances the experience.

Culinary Delights:

- Beachfront Dining:

Hideaway Island features beachfront dining options that offer a delectable array of local and international cuisines. Enjoy freshly caught seafood, tropical fruits, and traditional Vanuatu dishes while overlooking the panoramic vistas of the Pacific Ocean.

- Island Bar:

The island bar is a hub of social activity, serving refreshing tropical drinks and cocktails. It's an ideal spot to mingle with fellow travelers, share stories of underwater adventures, and bask in the camaraderie that defines Hideaway Island's communal spirit.

Cultural Experiences:

- Local Performances:

Embrace the cultural richness of Vanuatu with traditional dance and music performances held on the island. Local performers showcase the vibrant heritage of the Ni-Vanuatu people, creating an immersive experience for visitors.

- Island Tours:

For a deeper understanding of local culture, consider taking guided island tours. Visit nearby villages, interact with the locals, and gain insights into the traditional customs that have been passed down through generations.

Practical Tips for Visitors:

- Eco-Friendly Practices:

Hideaway Island is committed to sustainability, and visitors are encouraged to embrace eco-friendly practices. Respect the marine life, follow responsible snorkeling and diving guidelines, and participate in conservation efforts to preserve the pristine environment.

- Weather Considerations:

Vanuatu's tropical climate means that weather conditions can vary throughout the year. Check the weather forecast before planning your visit to ensure optimal conditions for both land and water activities.

- Reservations and Booking:

If you plan to stay overnight or engage in specific activities, it's advisable to make reservations in advance, especially during peak tourist seasons. This ensures that you secure your preferred accommodations and activities.

3.7 Blue Lagoon, Efate

Nestled on the western coast of Efate, the Blue Lagoon is a natural wonder that mesmerizes visitors with its crystal-clear waters and lush surroundings. Also known as the "Blue Hole," this idyllic spot is a popular destination for those seeking a serene escape into nature. The lagoon is formed by a combination of freshwater springs and the tidal movements of the Pacific Ocean, creating a stunning blend of aquamarine hues that beckon travelers to immerse themselves in its pristine waters.

Getting There

- From Port Vila: Most travelers begin their journey to the Blue Lagoon from Port Vila, the capital of Vanuatu, situated on the southern coast of Efate. The lagoon is approximately a 30-minute drive from Port Vila, making it an easily accessible day trip.
- Transport Options: Various transportation options are available, including guided tours, rental cars, and taxis. Guided tours often include informative commentary about the region, while rental cars provide flexibility for independent exploration.

What Makes the Blue Lagoon Unique?

- Crystal-Clear Waters:

The hallmark of the Blue Lagoon lies in its mesmerizing crystal-clear waters, setting it apart as a natural wonder. The clarity of the lagoon's waters is exceptional, granting visibility to the bottom even at considerable depths. This unparalleled transparency provides an immersive and surreal experience for swimmers and snorkelers alike. Whether wading in the shallows or exploring the deeper realms, visitors are enchanted by the pristine clarity that defines the Blue Lagoon's aquatic environment.

- Aquatic Life:

Beneath the surface of the Blue Lagoon, a vibrant and diverse world of marine life unfolds. Snorkelers are treated to a kaleidoscope of colors as they encounter intricate coral formations and tropical fish navigating the underwater landscape. The flourishing ecosystem within the lagoon adds an extra layer of wonder, allowing visitors to connect with the natural biodiversity that thrives in this unique environment.

- Surrounding Greenery:

Surrounded by lush greenery, the Blue Lagoon is embraced by the verdant beauty of Vanuatu. Towering trees and vibrant vegetation create a natural haven, providing shade and enhancing the peaceful ambiance of the surroundings. The lush green backdrop complements the azure waters, inviting visitors to unwind, relax, and appreciate the harmonious coexistence of land and water in this idyllic paradise. Whether basking in the sun, swinging from the rope, or simply soaking in the tranquility, the surrounding greenery adds to the enchantment of the Blue Lagoon, making it an ideal destination for nature lovers and adventure seekers alike.

Activities at the Blue Lagoon

- Swimming and Snorkeling:

The serene allure of the Blue Lagoon extends an irresistible invitation to visitors, urging them to embrace the refreshing embrace of its calm and clear waters. The lagoon serves as a natural swimming pool, offering a tranquil environment for those seeking a leisurely dip. However, the true magic lies beneath the surface, making snorkeling an absolute must for those eager to explore the underwater wonders. The vibrant coral formations, teeming with marine life, transform the Blue Lagoon into an underwater sanctuary waiting to be discovered.

- Tarzan Rope Swing Experience:

For the thrill-seekers and adventure enthusiasts, the Blue Lagoon presents an exhilarating experience with its Tarzan rope swing. Suspended from the overhanging trees, the rope swing provides an adrenaline-pumping opportunity to plunge into the lagoon's inviting waters. This dynamic activity not only adds a touch of excitement but also complements the serene setting, creating a perfect balance between adventure and tranquility.

- Picnicking and Relaxation:

The shores of the Blue Lagoon offer an idyllic setting for leisure and relaxation. Visitors can indulge in a leisurely picnic, bringing along snacks or a meal to enjoy amidst the natural beauty that surrounds them. Sunbathing on the soft sands, cooled by the gentle breeze, becomes a delightful pastime, allowing guests to absorb the breathtaking scenery and unwind in the lap of nature.

- Guided Tours and Cultural Experiences:

To deepen the Blue Lagoon experience, some visitors opt for guided tours that provide not only ecological insights into the area but also cultural enrichment. Knowledgeable guides share the ecological significance of the lagoon, shedding light on the delicate balance of the ecosystem. Furthermore, these tours often incorporate cultural experiences, offering a glimpse into the historical and customary aspects of the region. Learning about the traditions and customs associated with the Blue Lagoon adds layers of meaning to the visit, fostering a greater appreciation for the interconnectedness of nature and culture in this enchanting corner of Vanuatu.

3.8 Ratua Island

Ratua Island is a private paradise, part of the Vanuatu archipelago, situated in the Coral Sea. This exclusive island sanctuary spans over 146 acres, boasting white sandy beaches, lush tropical forests, and crystal-clear turquoise waters. The island is not only a haven for those seeking a secluded retreat but also a destination that emphasizes sustainable and eco-friendly tourism practices.

2. Geographical Marvels

- Beaches and Coastal Beauty

Ratua Island is a haven of coastal beauty, adorned with pristine beaches that offer a symphony of natural wonders. Each beach on the island boasts a unique ambiance, ranging from the soft, powdery sands of Coconut Beach to the rugged allure of Coral Beach's rocky outcrops. Visitors can meander along the shoreline, indulging in the tranquil atmosphere for a leisurely stroll or setting the stage for a romantic sunset dinner.

The warm, crystalline waters surrounding Ratua Island beckon snorkeling enthusiasts to explore vibrant marine life beneath the surface. Whether diving into the underwater world or simply reveling in the panoramic ocean views, the beaches of Ratua create an unparalleled backdrop for both relaxation and exploration.

- Tropical Fauna and Flora

Venturing into Ratua Island's interior reveals a lush tapestry of tropical vegetation, a sanctuary for an impressive array of native flora and fauna. Birdwatchers will find delight in spotting colorful parrots and exotic bird species, their vibrant plumage contrasting against the verdant foliage. Guided walks through the island's interior unveil the captivating diversity of plant life, showcasing the resilience and adaptability of species thriving in Ratua's tropical climate.

- Marine Life and Coral Reefs

For those captivated by the mysteries of the deep, Ratua Island offers unparalleled opportunities to explore marine life and coral reefs. The surrounding waters host thriving coral reefs, creating a mesmerizing underwater spectacle. Snorkelers can immerse themselves in an aquatic wonderland, encountering schools of vibrant fish, the graceful glide of sea turtles, and the kaleidoscopic hues of intricate coral formations. Ratua's commitment to marine conservation ensures that these underwater ecosystems remain vibrant and teeming with life, inviting visitors to witness the interconnected beauty of the island's coastal and aquatic realms.

3. Cultural Immersion on Ratua Island

- Indigenous Practices

Ratua Island embraces and celebrates Vanuatu's indigenous culture. Visitors have the chance to engage with the local community and participate in traditional practices. From witnessing customary dances to learning about age-old rituals, the cultural experiences on Ratua Island offer a genuine connection to the rich heritage of Vanuatu.

- Traditional Architecture

The accommodation on Ratua Island reflects a commitment to preserving local traditions. Guests can stay in beautifully crafted, traditional-style villas constructed from sustainable, locally-sourced materials. These villas not only provide luxurious comfort but also showcase the artistry of Vanuatu's traditional architecture.

4. Accommodation on Ratua Island

- Overwater Bungalows

Ratua Island offers a range of accommodation options, including exquisite overwater bungalows that allow guests to wake up to the gentle lapping of waves beneath their private oasis. These traditional-style bungalows seamlessly blend luxury with authenticity, providing an unparalleled stay on the water.

- Private Villas

For those seeking a more secluded experience, the island boasts private villas nestled within lush gardens, offering privacy and tranquility. Each villa is tastefully decorated with local artifacts and provides a harmonious balance between modern amenities and traditional charm.

5. Activities on Ratua Island

- Water-based Adventures

Ratua Island offers an array of water-based activities, from kayaking through mangrove forests to sailing on traditional outrigger canoes. Snorkeling and diving excursions allow guests to explore the vibrant underwater world surrounding the island, while deep-sea fishing trips offer a chance to catch the local bounty.

- Equestrian Experiences

For a unique adventure, Ratua Island provides equestrian activities on its expansive grounds. Guests can embark on guided horseback rides, exploring the island's interior and coastline while enjoying breathtaking views and connecting with nature in a truly immersive way.

- Spa and Wellness Retreats

To complement the island's natural beauty, Ratua offers spa and wellness retreats. Indulge in rejuvenating treatments amidst the tranquil surroundings, providing a holistic experience that combines relaxation with the serenity of the island.

6. Sustainability and Responsible Tourism

Ratua Island is committed to sustainable and responsible tourism practices. From eco-friendly construction methods to community engagement initiatives, the island strives to minimize its environmental impact while contributing positively to the local community. Visitors are encouraged to participate in these initiatives, fostering a sense of responsibility towards the environment and cultural preservation.

3.9 Pele Island

Pele Island, also known as Fao, is a small, charming island situated just off the northern coast of Efate, Vanuatu's main island. This hidden gem is a haven for those seeking tranquility, natural beauty, and a glimpse into the authentic island way of life. Accessible by a short boat ride from the mainland, Pele Island promises a serene escape surrounded by turquoise waters and lush landscapes.

Getting to Pele Island:

Your adventure to Pele Island begins with a scenic boat journey, typically departing from Emua Village on the northeast coast of Efate. Boats operated by local guides offer a picturesque voyage, allowing you to soak in the breathtaking views of the Pacific Ocean. The short journey enhances the anticipation, setting the stage for the tropical paradise awaiting you.

Natural Wonders and Beach Bliss:

- Sandy Beaches and Crystal Clear Waters:

Pele Island's pristine allure is epitomized by its stretches of immaculate, white sandy beaches that caress the coastline, creating an ideal haven for relaxation and rejuvenation. The crystal-clear waters gently lap at the shore, beckoning you to immerse yourself in a world of aquatic bliss. Whether you choose to revel in the sheer delight of swimming, embark on an enchanting snorkeling expedition, or simply lounge under the sun, Pele Island's beaches offer a timeless escape. The tranquil ambiance, accompanied by the soothing sounds of the ocean and the rustling of palm trees, creates an atmosphere where time itself seems to slow down, allowing you to embrace the serenity of this tropical sanctuary.

- Coral Gardens and Snorkeling:

Venture beneath the surface, and Pele Island reveals a mesmerizing marine wonderland. The coral gardens encircling the island are teeming with an array of vibrant fish and other captivating marine life. For snorkeling enthusiasts, this underwater paradise offers an immersive experience, where you can navigate through intricate coral formations and encounter a diverse array of marine species. For those seeking deeper insights, guided snorkeling tours are readily available, providing expert commentary and enhancing your appreciation for the aquatic treasures that adorn Pele Island's vibrant underwater realm. As you submerge yourself in these crystal-clear waters, you'll find that Pele Island's underwater landscapes are as enchanting as the pristine shores that grace its surface.

Cultural Encounters:

- Local Villages and Community Engagement:

Pele Island beckons travelers to partake in a cultural odyssey by offering a unique opportunity to immerse themselves in the vibrant life of its local villages. As you step into these charming communities, a warm welcome awaits from the islanders, eager to share their traditions and stories. Engaging with the locals provides an authentic glimpse into their daily lives, allowing you to forge meaningful connections. Wander through the village pathways, interact with residents, and consider participating in cultural activities that unveil the island's heritage. The rhythmic beats of traditional dances may resonate in the air, inviting you to witness and appreciate the rich tapestry of Pele Island's cultural legacy.

- Local Cuisine and Culinary Experiences:

Elevate your cultural journey by savoring the delectable flavors of Pele Island's local cuisine. Islanders generously share their culinary heritage, offering a tantalizing array of dishes that showcase the region's gastronomic traditions. Indulge in the freshest seafood delicacies and tropical fruits, each bite a celebration of Vanuatu's rich culinary diversity. Engaging in a communal meal with the locals not only adds a delightful touch to your cultural experience but also creates a shared space where stories are exchanged, fostering a deeper understanding of the island's people and their connection to the bountiful land and sea that sustain their vibrant way of life.

Adventure and Exploration:

- Hiking and Nature Trails:

Pele Island unfolds as a paradise for those seeking adventure, with its lush interior inviting exploration through hiking and nature trails. Embark on a journey through the heart of the island, where verdant landscapes and diverse flora and fauna paint the canvas of the natural world. The trailblazing experience allows you to immerse yourself in the rich biodiversity of Pele Island, discovering hidden pockets of botanical wonders and encountering indigenous wildlife. Guided hikes elevate the experience, offering informative insights into the island's ecosystem, turning every step into a revelation for nature enthusiasts. Traverse the enchanting trails, breathe in the crisp island air, and let the spirit of adventure guide you through Pele Island's captivating interior.

- Exploring Blue Lagoons:

Pele Island unveils hidden treasures in the form of serene blue lagoons and secluded coves, scattered like gems across its landscape. These tranquil havens provide a welcome escape, surrounded by the untouched beauty of nature. Whether you choose to gracefully kayak through the calm waters or prefer a leisurely stroll along the pristine shoreline, the blue lagoons of Pele Island beckon as enchanting retreats. The azure hues of the lagoons, complemented by the verdant backdrop, create a picturesque setting, inviting you to unwind, connect with nature, and relish the tranquility that defines Pele Island's secluded paradises.

Practical Tips for Visiting Pele Island:

1. Boat Tours and Guides:

Ensure a seamless journey by arranging boat tours with reputable local guides. These guides not only navigate the waters safely but also share their intimate knowledge of Pele Island, enhancing your overall experience.

2. Respect for Local Culture:

When engaging with the local communities, display cultural sensitivity and respect for traditions. Seek permission before taking photographs and participate in cultural exchanges with an open and appreciative mindset.

3. Environmental Stewardship:

Preserve the pristine beauty of Pele Island by practicing responsible tourism. Respect the natural environment, follow designated trails, and adhere to waste disposal guidelines to minimize your ecological footprint.

4. Snorkeling Equipment:

Bring your snorkeling gear or check with local operators for equipment rental options. Exploring Pele Island's coral reefs is a memorable experience, and having the right equipment enhances your underwater adventure.

3.10 Ekasup Cultural Village

1. Introduction to Ekasup Cultural Village

Ekasup Cultural Village, situated near Port Vila, Vanuatu's capital, serves as a captivating microcosm of Ni-Vanuatu heritage. This living cultural haven beckons visitors to embark on a time-traveling adventure, immersing themselves in the vibrant traditions, age-old rituals, and the authentic daily life of indigenous communities. As a living museum of Vanuatu's cultural richness, Ekasup Cultural Village provides a unique opportunity to connect with the heart and soul of the Ni-Vanuatu people, fostering a profound understanding of their enduring traditions in a modern world.

2. Getting There and Admission

Conveniently nestled just a short drive from Port Vila, Ekasup Cultural Village is easily accessible for curious travelers. Many hotels and resorts offer guided tours to Ekasup, ensuring a seamless experience with transportation to and from the village. Upon arrival, the warmth of the local community envelops visitors as friendly locals guide them through the immersive cultural experience.

Admission fees to Ekasup are typically reasonable, allowing visitors to gain a profound understanding of Ni-Vanuatu heritage without breaking the bank. To stay informed, it's advisable to check with tour operators or directly with the village for the most up-to-date information on fees and any additional offerings. Some tour packages may even include captivating traditional performances, offering a comprehensive and enriching exploration of Vanuatu's cultural tapestry.

3. Village Layout and Architecture

Designed to authentically mirror a traditional Ni-Vanuatu community, Ekasup Cultural Village showcases the timeless charm of thatched roof huts and open-air structures. The layout meticulously captures the essence of communal living, a hallmark of Ni-Vanuatu life for centuries. As visitors meander through the village, they embark on a journey through time, witnessing the architectural authenticity that defines Ekasup. The thatched roofs and open layouts not only provide a glimpse into the historical living arrangements but also immerse guests in the cultural legacy of the Ni-Vanuatu people. This well-crafted village layout serves as a living canvas, preserving and narrating the rich cultural heritage of Vanuatu in every intricately designed structure.

4. Cultural Exhibitions and Activities

1 Traditional Dance Performances

At Ekasup Cultural Village, the beating heart of Ni-Vanuatu culture comes alive through vibrant traditional dance performances. Renowned for their captivating displays, visitors are treated to an immersive experience of intricate dance forms adorned with traditional costumes and accompanied by rhythmic drumming. These performances are not merely a spectacle; they are a living expression of the artistic prowess of the Ni-Vanuatu people. Each dance narrates stories steeped in history and cultural significance, creating a dynamic and visual journey that bridges the past and the present.

2 Storytelling Sessions

Elders and esteemed community leaders at Ekasup engage visitors in enchanting storytelling sessions, weaving tales passed down through generations. These stories serve as windows into the rich oral tradition of the Ni-Vanuatu people, offering profound insights into their beliefs, customs, and the profound interconnectedness between humanity and nature. As visitors sit enthralled, the narratives unfold, creating a tapestry that connects the listener with the deep roots of Ni-Vanuatu heritage.

3 Customary Demonstrations

A true highlight of Ekasup Cultural Village is the opportunity to witness customary demonstrations of everyday activities. From traditional cooking methods that have sustained Ni-Vanuatu communities for generations to the intricate artistry of handicrafts and the nuanced techniques of fishing, visitors gain firsthand experience in the essential skills that define daily life in Vanuatu. This authentic showcase allows guests to appreciate the resilience and resourcefulness embedded in the fabric of Ni-Vanuatu culture.

4 Interactive Workshops

For those seeking a more hands-on and immersive experience, Ekasup Cultural Village offers interactive workshops. Here, visitors can actively participate in various cultural activities, such as weaving intricate patterns, learning the delicate art of traditional face painting, or trying their hand at playing the melodic tunes of traditional musical instruments. These workshops not only provide a unique opportunity for cultural exchange but also foster a personal connection with the local community, creating memorable moments of shared learning and appreciation.

In essence, Ekasup Cultural Village transcends the conventional tourist experience by offering a multifaceted exploration of Ni Vanuatu heritage. From the rhythmic beats of traditional dances to the timeless tales shared in storytelling sessions, and from the skilled demonstrations of everyday activities to the interactive workshops that invite participation, Ekasup ensures that every visitor departs with a profound understanding of Vanuatu's rich cultural legacy.

5. Cultural Etiquette and Respectful Tourism

1 Respecting Traditional Practices

Visitors are encouraged to embrace the principles of responsible tourism and respect the cultural practices of the Ni-Vanuatu people. Engaging in cultural activities with an open mind and a willingness to learn fosters mutual understanding and appreciation.

2 Photography Etiquette

While Ekasup Cultural Village welcomes photography, it's essential to seek permission before capturing images of individuals or specific ceremonies. Some customs may have restrictions on photography, and respecting these guidelines ensures a respectful and considerate visit.

6. Practical Tips for Visitors

1 Dress Code

Given the cultural significance of the village, visitors are advised to dress modestly. Lightweight, comfortable clothing, preferably covering the shoulders and knees, is recommended out of respect for traditional values.

2 Footwear

As a sign of respect and to maintain the cleanliness of the village, visitors are often asked to remove their shoes before entering traditional huts or participating in certain activities. Wearing slip-on shoes or sandals makes this process more convenient.

3 Language Considerations

While many locals at Ekasup Cultural Village may speak English, learning a few basic phrases in Bislama, the local Creole language, can enhance the cultural exchange and communication with the Ni-Vanuatu people.

4 Purchasing Handicrafts

Ekasup Cultural Village often offers visitors the chance to purchase handmade crafts and souvenirs. By buying directly from the artisans, visitors contribute to the local economy and support the continuation of traditional craftsmanship.

3.11 Chief Roi Mata's Domain

1. Understanding Chief Roi Mata's Legacy:

Chief Roi Mata, a luminary figure in Vanuatu's history, exerted profound influence in molding the cultural and social fabric of the archipelago. In the late 16th century, his leadership left an enduring imprint on the Ni-Vanuatu people. His visionary approach emphasized unity and peace, fostering harmony among diverse tribes and laying the groundwork for a cohesive society. This forward-thinking perspective not only ensured the stability of the time but also sowed the seeds for the distinctive cultural identity that

Vanuatu cherished to this day. Chief Roi Mata's legacy is a testament to the transformative power of leadership in shaping the destinies of nations and preserving the cultural heritage that defines their essence.

2. The UNESCO World Heritage Site:

Designated as a UNESCO World Heritage Site in 2008, Chief Roi Mata's Domain stands as a testament to its exceptional universal value. This recognition underscores the significance of the site in preserving and showcasing the cultural heritage of Vanuatu. The domain comprises three integral areas: the serene Artok Island, the sacred Fels Cave on Lelepa Island, and the poignant burial grounds on Hat Island. Together, these locations form a comprehensive representation of Chief Roi Mata's domain, offering a unique insight into the spiritual and ceremonial dimensions of traditional Ni-Vanuatu society. Visitors to Chief Roi Mata's Domain have the privilege of immersing themselves in a living history, experiencing the cultural richness and profound legacy that has earned this site its esteemed place on the global stage.

3. The Island of Artok:

Nestled in the embrace of the South Pacific, the tranquil Artok Island serves as the poignant final resting place of Chief Roi Mata. As visitors step onto this small and picturesque island, they embark on a journey through time, exploring the sacred grounds where the chief was laid to rest. The site offers a profound insight into the customs and rituals entwined with the passing of a paramount leader, creating a reflective atmosphere amidst the pristine surroundings. The tranquility of Artok fosters a connection with the spiritual significance of the site, inviting visitors to pay homage to Chief Roi Mata and witness the sacred beauty that encapsulates his eternal abode.

4. Fels Cave on Lelepa Island:

Venturing to Lelepa Island unveils the mystique of Fels Cave, a sacred site of deep ceremonial importance within Chief Roi Mata's Domain. This cave, adorned with intricate rock art, stands as a testament to ancient burial rituals and spiritual practices of the Ni-Vanuatu people. As visitors explore the depths of Fels Cave, they encounter a gallery of time-honored expressions, witnessing the symbolic legacy that once played a pivotal role in the cultural tapestry of Vanuatu. The cave's ethereal ambiance and the preserved rock art create an immersive experience, allowing modern travelers to connect with the artistic and spiritual dimensions that defined the era of Chief Roi Mata.

5. Hat Island Burial Grounds:

As the journey through Chief Roi Mata's Domain continues, Hat Island unfolds as the poignant keeper of the burial grounds for those connected to Chief Roi Mata's court. Here, the landscape whispers tales of an era gone by, revealing the elaborate burial customs of the time. Carefully arranged stones, each a silent sentinel, mark the resting places of individuals who played significant roles within the chief's domain. The site on Hat Island stands as a testament to the reverence and respect bestowed upon those entrusted with important positions, offering visitors a somber yet insightful glimpse into the cultural practices of Chief Roi Mata's era.

6. Preservation Efforts:

Preserving the sanctity of Chief Roi Mata's Domain is a collaborative endeavor that unites local communities, governmental bodies, and international organizations in a shared commitment to safeguarding this invaluable cultural heritage. Comprehensive conservation initiatives are in place, diligently focusing on maintaining the integrity of the sites, preventing erosion, and ensuring the longevity of these historical landscapes. Educational programs and community engagement initiatives play a pivotal role in fostering awareness and appreciation, contributing significantly to the sustainable preservation of this UNESCO-listed site. Through collective efforts, the legacy of Chief Roi Mata is not only preserved for present generations but is also passed on responsibly to future custodians of this unique and culturally significant heritage.

7. Immersive Experiences for Visitors:

Exploring Chief Roi Mata's Domain goes beyond admiring archaeological sites; it offers a chance for visitors to engage in immersive experiences that bring the history and culture to life.

- Guided Tours: Knowledgeable local guides provide insights into Chief Roi Mata's life, the historical context of his reign, and the cultural significance of the sites. These guided tours enhance the visitor's understanding of the complex social structures and rituals associated with Chief Roi Mata's era.
- Cultural Performances: Some tours include traditional dance performances and storytelling sessions, offering

visitors a vibrant and interactive experience. These cultural performances showcase the living traditions inspired by Chief Roi Mata's legacy.

- Community Interaction: Engaging with local communities near Chief Roi Mata's Domain provides a deeper cultural immersion. Visitors may have the opportunity to participate in community events, try traditional foods, and witness the ongoing preservation efforts led by the Ni-Vanuatu people.

8. Practical Tips for Visitors:

- Guided Tours: Opting for guided tours ensures a comprehensive understanding of the historical and cultural nuances associated with Chief Roi Mata's Domain. Local guides often share personal stories, enriching the visitor experience.
- Respectful Conduct: Visitors are encouraged to approach these sacred sites with respect and mindfulness. This includes adhering to any guidelines provided by guides or site authorities to preserve the cultural integrity of Chief Roi Mata's Domain.
- Comfortable Attire: As exploration may involve walking or hiking, wearing comfortable and modest attire, along with sturdy footwear, is advisable. Be prepared for varying terrain and weather conditions.
- Photography: While photography is often permitted, it's essential to confirm the guidelines at each site. Respecting any restrictions on photography helps maintain the sanctity of the cultural and spiritual spaces.

3.12 Nanda Blue Hole

1. Introduction to Nanda Blue Hole: A Natural Wonder

- Location and Accessibility:

Nanda Blue Hole graces Espiritu Santo, Vanuatu's largest island, reachable from Luganville, the island's primary town. The journey to Nanda Blue Hole unfolds as an adventure, meandering through scenic drives enveloped in lush jungles. En route, visitors traverse local villages and picturesque landscapes, heightening the anticipation for the hidden gem that awaits at the end of the road.

- The Pristine Beauty of Nanda Blue Hole:

Nanda Blue Hole, a natural freshwater spring, is embraced by tropical foliage, creating an enchanting oasis. The crystalline waters unveil a spectrum of blues, weaving a mesmerizing underwater world. Fed by an intricate underground network of springs, the pool ensures a constant flow of refreshing water, inviting visitors to immerse themselves in the pristine and rejuvenating embrace of this natural wonder.

2. Planning Your Visit to Nanda Blue Hole

- Best Time to Visit

Vanuatu enjoys a tropical climate, and the best time to visit Nanda Blue Hole is during the dry season, which typically runs from May to October. This period ensures clear skies and ideal conditions for swimming and underwater exploration. However, keep in mind that this is a popular tourist destination, so arriving early in the day can provide a more tranquil experience.

- Entry Fees and Permits

To maintain the pristine condition of Nanda Blue Hole, a small entry fee is usually required. This fee contributes to the conservation efforts and supports the local communities. It's advisable to check the current entry fees and inquire about any necessary permits before embarking on your journey.

3. The Nanda Blue Hole Experience

- Swimming and Snorkeling:

The allure of Nanda Blue Hole extends beyond its enchanting surface, inviting tourists into its crystal-clear embrace. The refreshing pool beckons visitors to immerse themselves in its azure depths, creating a serene and invigorating experience. For snorkeling enthusiasts, Nanda Blue Hole unveils a mesmerizing underwater world. With exceptional visibility, snorkelers can closely encounter the vibrant marine life that inhabits the spring, providing an immersive exploration of the aquatic wonders beneath the surface.

- Rope Swings and Tarzan Adventures:

Nanda Blue Hole caters to adventure seekers with the thrill of rope swings strategically positioned around the pool. Offering a Tarzan-like experience, visitors can swing from these ropes, creating an exhilarating sensation as they plunge into the pristine waters below. This perfect fusion of natural beauty and adventurous fun adds a dynamic element to the Nanda Blue Hole experience, making it an ideal destination for those seeking an adrenaline rush amidst the tranquility of nature.

- Picnicking in Paradise:

Beyond the aquatic adventures, Nanda Blue Hole provides an idyllic setting for a leisurely picnic, elevating the visitor experience. Guests have the option to bring along a packed lunch or indulge in local delights available from nearby vendors. Shaded areas and wooden platforms offer a comfortable spot to relax, savor the beauty of the surroundings, and relish a delightful picnic in this tropical paradise. Whether it's the thrill of adventure or the tranquility of a picnic, Nanda Blue Hole caters to diverse tastes, ensuring a memorable visit for every traveler.

4. Respectful Tourism: Preserving Nanda Blue Hole

- Responsible Tourism Practices

Preserving the natural integrity of Nanda Blue Hole is essential for future generations to enjoy. Tourists are encouraged to practice responsible tourism by refraining from littering, respecting local flora and fauna, and following any guidelines provided by the local authorities.

- Supporting Local Communities

When visiting Nanda Blue Hole, consider supporting the local communities surrounding this natural wonder. Purchase handmade crafts or goods from local vendors, contributing directly to the livelihoods of the people who call Espiritu Santo home.

5. Practical Tips for a Memorable Visit

- What to Bring

To ensure a comfortable and enjoyable visit, tourists should consider bringing essentials such as swimwear, sunscreen, insect repellent, and a reusable water bottle. A waterproof camera is also recommended to capture the vivid underwater scenes.

- Guided Tours

For those who prefer a guided experience, there are local tour operators offering excursions to Nanda Blue Hole. These guided tours often include transportation, entry fees, and additional insights into the natural and cultural aspects of the region.

- Weather Considerations

While the dry season is generally the best time to visit, weather conditions can change. It's advisable to check the weather forecast before planning your trip to ensure optimal conditions for a memorable experience.

3.13 Tetamanu Village

1. Introduction to Tetamanu Village

Situated on one of Vanuatu's numerous islands, Tetamanu Village is a charming enclave that epitomizes the authenticity and cultural richness of the archipelago. Its name, resonating with historical significance, is derived from traditional Ni-Vanuatu language, embodying the deep connection the villagers maintain with their ancestral roots. For travelers seeking an escape from the bustling modern world and a genuine encounter with Vanuatu's indigenous way of life, Tetamanu Village emerges as a must-visit destination.

2. Getting to Tetamanu Village

Before embarking on the journey to Tetamanu Village, it's essential to plan your travel logistics. The village is accessible via boat from various points on the island, and most tours to Tetamanu depart from major hubs like Port Vila or Luganville. Visitors can opt for guided tours that often include a scenic boat ride, providing glimpses of Vanuatu's coastal beauty before reaching the shores of Tetamanu. Be sure to check with local tour operators for availability and departure schedules.

3. Accommodations in Tetamanu Village

While Tetamanu Village is not typically known for large resorts, it offers a unique opportunity for travelers to experience traditional Ni-Vanuatu hospitality through homestays. Local families open their homes to visitors, providing an immersive cultural experience. Staying in a traditional village setting allows tourists to connect with the community, learn about customs firsthand, and gain insights into the daily lives of the Ni-Vanuatu people.

4. Cultural Immersion in Tetamanu Village

- Traditional Practices and Customs

Tetamanu Village provides an authentic window into the traditional practices and customs of the Ni-Vanuatu people. From ancient rituals to daily activities, visitors can witness the villagers engaging in customary practices that have been passed down through generations. Traditional dances, ceremonies, and storytelling sessions offer an intimate connection to the vibrant cultural heritage of Tetamanu.

- Participating in Village Life

Travelers are encouraged to actively engage with the local community, participating in various village activities. This could include trying your hand at traditional crafts, assisting in farming activities, or even joining in the preparation of a local meal. Such interactions foster meaningful connections and contribute to a more enriching travel experience.

5. Exploring Tetamanu's Natural Beauty

1 Beachside Bliss: Tropical Tranquility

Tetamanu's pristine beaches, adorned with powdery white sand and kissed by crystal-clear turquoise waters, create a haven of serenity. Travelers can unwind under the shade of gently swaying coconut palms, letting the rhythmic sound of the waves create a soothing backdrop. Whether you prefer lounging with a good book, taking a leisurely stroll along the shore, or immersing yourself in water activities like snorkeling, Tetamanu's coastal beauty invites you to indulge in moments of bliss along the warm Pacific waters.

2 Hiking Trails and Nature Walks: Adventure Awaits

For those with an adventurous spirit, Tetamanu Village unveils a treasure trove of exploration within the lush interior of the island. Expertly guided hiking trails wind through dense rainforests, offering glimpses of exotic flora and fauna. These trails often lead to scenic viewpoints where travelers can stand in awe of panoramic vistas, immersing themselves in the untamed beauty of Tetamanu's natural landscapes.

3 Cultural Landmarks: Unveiling History and Spirituality

Tetamanu is not only a haven of natural beauty but also a repository of cultural landmarks that tell the story of the village's rich history and spirituality. Visitors are invited to explore traditional meeting grounds, ancient ceremonial sites, and other significant landmarks. Local guides, with their wealth of knowledge, provide insights into the cultural significance of each site, offering a deeper understanding of Tetamanu's heritage. Immerse yourself in the living history of the village as you discover the sacred sites that contribute to the unique tapestry of Tetamanu's cultural

6. Culinary Delights in Tetamanu Village

1 Traditional Ni-Vanuatu Cuisine

Tetamanu Village offers a delectable introduction to traditional Ni-Vanuatu cuisine. Visitors can savor local delicacies prepared by skilled village cooks, experiencing the flavors of freshly caught seafood, tropical fruits, and indigenous vegetables. Engaging in communal meals provides not only a gastronomic adventure but also a chance to bond with the local community over shared culinary traditions.

2 Food Experiences and Cooking Classes

For those keen on a more immersive culinary experience, some homestays in Tetamanu Village may offer cooking classes. Participants can learn to prepare traditional dishes, gaining insights into the unique ingredients and cooking techniques that define Ni-Vanuatu cuisine.

3.14 Ambrym Island - Land of Volcanoes

Nestled in the heart of the Vanuatu archipelago, Ambrym Island stands as a mesmerizing testament to the raw power of nature. Renowned as the "Land of Volcanoes," Ambrym is a captivating destination that beckons adventurous travelers seeking an immersive encounter with both the cultural and geological wonders of the South Pacific. In this comprehensive guide, we will explore the allure of Ambrym, from its volcanic landscapes and unique cultural practices to practical travel tips for an unforgettable journey.

Discovering Ambrym's Volcanic Landscape

1. Mount Marum and Mount Benbow: The Dynamic Duo

Ambrym's allure lies in the formidable presence of two of the world's most active and accessible volcanoes—Mount Marum and Mount Benbow. These colossal giants stand as geological sentinels, their imposing figures dominating the island's landscape and serving as a visceral reminder of the Earth's primal forces. Embarking on a trek to the rim of these majestic volcanoes provides an unparalleled adventure. As you ascend, the surreal experience unfolds—peering into the cauldrons of boiling lava, witnessing otherworldly landscapes, and feeling the earth's tremors beneath your feet. This immersive encounter with the raw, untamed power of nature on Ambrym is a journey into the heart of the Earth itself, an experience etched forever in the memory of intrepid travelers.

Tips for Volcanic Exploration:

- Guided Tours: Due to the potentially hazardous conditions, it's recommended to undertake volcano tours with experienced local guides who are familiar with the terrain and safety protocols.
- Safety Gear: Wear appropriate clothing, sturdy hiking boots, and carry essentials like a gas mask to protect against volcanic gases, especially when venturing close to active craters.

2. Yahul Custom Village: Cultural Immersion

Beyond its volcanic wonders, Ambrym boasts a rich cultural tapestry, notably exemplified in the traditional villages like Yahul. This village provides a rare opportunity to witness age-old customs, traditional dances, and the unique artistry of the island's inhabitants. From mesmerizing sand drawings to the haunting rhythms of tam-tams (traditional slit gongs), Yahul offers a glimpse into the soul of Ambrym's indigenous culture.

- Cultural Insights: Tam-Tams and Rituals

Delve into the heart of Ambrym's indigenous culture through Tam-Tam ceremonies, where ancient instruments convey messages and commemorate significant events. Engage with locals in these rhythmic rituals to experience the profound spiritual connection embedded in every beat, revealing the island's deep-rooted traditions and communal bonds.

- Custom Dances

Immerse yourself in the cultural vibrancy of Ambrym by attending traditional dances. Villagers, adorned in customary attire, perform intricate movements that serve as living narratives, recounting the island's rich history and beliefs. These mesmerizing dance performances not only showcase the artistic expression of the locals but also offer a unique opportunity to connect with Ambrym's cultural heritage, fostering a deeper appreciation for the island's traditions.

Practical Travel Tips for Ambrym

1. Getting There:

Access to Ambrym is primarily through the country's capital, Port Vila. Domestic flights from Bauerfield International Airport to Craig Cove Airport in Ambrym are available. The journey itself is an aerial spectacle, providing stunning views of the archipelago and Ambrym's volcanic peaks.

2. Accommodations:

While Ambrym offers limited accommodation options compared to more tourist-centric destinations, there are guesthouses and bungalows that provide a comfortable stay. It's advisable to book accommodations in advance, especially during peak tourist seasons.

3. Local Transportation:

Ambrym's local transportation primarily involves walking, and some villages may require traversing challenging terrains. It's essential to be prepared for trekking and arrange for local guides to navigate safely through the island's diverse landscapes.

4. Weather Considerations:

Ambrym experiences a tropical climate with distinct wet and dry seasons. The best time to visit is during the dry season from May to October when the weather is more predictable, and volcanic activities are often more visible.

5. Cultural Sensitivity:

Respect for local customs is paramount. Seek permission before taking photographs, be mindful of traditional ceremonies, and participate with reverence. Understanding and appreciating the local way of life enriches the overall travel experience.

CHAPTER FOUR

NAVIGATING VANUATU

4.1 Transportation Options

Vanuatu, with its scattered archipelago of 83 islands in the South Pacific, offers a variety of transportation options to suit different preferences and destinations. Here's a breakdown of the various ways to get around in this tropical paradise:

4.1.1 Taxis:

For tourists venturing into the paradisiacal realm of Vanuatu, understanding the nuances of transportation is paramount for a seamless and enjoyable experience. Taxis, serving as convenient and versatile modes of travel, play a crucial role in facilitating mobility across the islands. Here's everything you need to know about using taxis in Vanuatu:

1. Urban Centers and Beyond:

- Availability: Taxis are readily available in major urban centers, particularly in places like Port Vila. Look for them near popular tourist spots, accommodations, and transportation hubs.
- Convenience: Hailing a taxi is a straightforward process. Simply raise your hand or head to a designated taxi stand, and you'll find a reliable means of getting around the city or town.

2. Airport Transfers:

- Efficient Transitions: Taxis are commonly employed for airport transfers, ensuring a smooth journey to or from the airport. Taxis are stationed at key airport locations, providing a hassle-free option for travelers arriving or departing from Bauerfield International Airport in Port Vila and other airports across the archipelago.
- Cost and Duration: While fares may vary, taxi rides offer a comfortable and time-efficient alternative for airport transfers, especially for those with limited time or carrying luggage.

3. Fares and Payment:

- Negotiation: Taxis in Vanuatu generally operate on a negotiable fare basis, so it's advisable to confirm the fare with the driver before starting your journey. Rates may vary, and it's common to discuss the fare upfront.
- Currency: Vanuatu uses the Vanuatu Vatu (VUV) as its official currency. Ensure you have local currency on hand, as not all taxis may accept credit cards.

4.1.2 Buses:

When it comes to immersing yourself in the vibrant local culture and scenic beauty of Vanuatu, buses emerge as an integral and authentic mode of transportation. For tourists eager to experience the rhythm of daily life, here is a comprehensive guide to navigating the islands via buses.

Local Buses: A Kaleidoscope of Color and Culture

Vanuatu's local buses are not just a means of transportation; they are a cultural experience in themselves. Decorated with vibrant colors, local art, and often accompanied by lively music, these buses provide a unique window into the heart of Vanuatu. In urban areas like Port Vila and Luganville, tourists can easily spot these distinctive vehicles lining the streets.

To board a local bus, simply flag one down from the side of the road and let the adventure begin. While routes may not always be clearly marked, friendly locals and bus conductors are usually more than happy to assist tourists in finding the right bus for their destination. The journey becomes an immersive experience as you share the space with locals, giving you an authentic taste of Vanuatu's community spirit.

Intercity Buses: Connecting Towns and Beyond

For travelers looking to venture beyond the city limits, intercity buses provide a reliable means of connecting towns and exploring the broader landscapes of Vanuatu. These buses operate on longer routes, offering both comfort and a chance to soak in the picturesque scenery. From Port Vila to Luganville and beyond, intercity buses are a gateway to diverse experiences.

To embark on an intercity journey, head to the designated bus terminals or inquire with your accommodation provider for guidance. While the travel duration might be longer than shorter local routes, the intercity bus experience allows you to witness the changing landscapes and connect with the charm of Vanuatu's rural areas.

Practical Tips for Bus Travel: Embracing the Adventure

- Payment: Bus fares are usually paid in cash directly to the bus conductor. It's advisable to carry smaller denominations to facilitate transactions.
- Schedules: Local buses often operate on a more flexible schedule, so it's helpful to check with locals or your accommodation for estimated departure times.
- Interactions: Engage with fellow passengers and the bus conductor. Locals are often eager to share insights, recommend attractions, and make your journey more enjoyable.
- Scenic Routes: Sit back and enjoy the views. Vanuatu's roads offer glimpses of lush landscapes, pristine beaches, and the vibrant colors of local life.

4.1.3 Rental Cars:

Here's everything you need to know about renting a car in Vanuatu:

1. Rental Car Availability:

- Urban Areas: In major urban centers like Port Vila, Luganville, and Lenakel, rental car agencies offer a variety of vehicles to suit different preferences and group sizes. These agencies are often conveniently located near airports and popular tourist hubs.
- Remote Islands: While rental cars may be less common on some remote islands, certain accommodations provide rental services or can assist in arranging transportation options suitable for the specific destination.

2. Driving in Vanuatu:

- Road Conditions: In urban areas, roads are generally well-maintained, but on remote islands, conditions may vary. Be prepared for a mix of sealed and unsealed roads, and consider the type of vehicle that suits your intended destinations.
- Traffic Rules: Vanuatu follows the British system of driving on the left side of the road. Familiarize yourself with local traffic rules, speed limits, and road signs.

3. Rental Car Options:

- Vehicle Types: Rental car agencies offer a range of vehicles, from compact cars for city exploration to larger SUVs for off-road adventures. Choose a vehicle that aligns with your travel plans and group size.
- Additional Features: Some agencies provide extras such as GPS navigation systems, child seats, and roof racks. Inquire about these options when making your reservation.

4. Rental Requirements:

- Driver's License: International visitors are required to have a valid driver's license from their home country. Driving permits are not necessary unless staying for an extended period.
- Age Restrictions: Most rental agencies have a minimum age requirement for drivers, typically 21 or 25 years old. Younger drivers may need to pay an additional fee.

5. Booking in Advance:

- Online Reservations: To ensure availability and secure the best rates, consider booking your rental car online before arriving in Vanuatu. Many agencies have user-friendly websites that facilitate easy reservations.
- On-Site Rentals: While booking in advance is recommended, on-site rentals are often possible, especially in urban areas. However, availability may be limited during peak tourist seasons.

Renting a car in Vanuatu grants you the autonomy to explore its stunning landscapes, from pristine beaches to lush rainforests, at your own pace. With careful planning and an understanding of local driving conditions, a rental car becomes your ticket to uncovering the hidden gems and natural wonders of this Pacific haven.

4.1.4 Ferries and Boats:

For the intrepid traveler seeking to explore the myriad islands of Vanuatu, ferries and boats become more than just modes of transportation—they are gateways to hidden coves, pristine beaches, and the untouched beauty of the Pacific Ocean. Understanding the nuances of maritime travel is key to unlocking the full potential of your Vanuatu adventure.

1. Island-Hopping Adventures:

Ferries and boats serve as vital links connecting the diverse islands of Vanuatu. Regular ferry services crisscross the archipelago, offering tourists the opportunity to embark on captivating island-hopping adventures. From the bustling streets of Port Vila on Efate to the more secluded corners of

Tanna or Espiritu Santo, these waterborne journeys provide not only a means of transportation but also a front-row seat to the breathtaking natural landscapes that define Vanuatu.

2. Scenic Routes and Secluded Destinations:

One of the highlights of opting for ferries and boats is the chance to revel in the scenic beauty that surrounds you. As the vessels navigate the azure waters, passengers are treated to panoramic views of lush greenery, coral reefs, and volcanic landscapes. Remote destinations that may be inaccessible by other means of transport become accessible, opening up a world of exploration for those seeking a more immersive experience.

3. Practical Information for Tourists:

Schedules and Routes:

- Familiarize yourself with ferry schedules and routes in advance. Schedules may vary based on the day of the week and the specific island destinations.
- Confirm departure and arrival points to ensure you board the correct ferry for your intended destination.

Ticketing and Reservations:

- Purchase ferry tickets in advance, especially during peak travel times. This guarantees you a seat and avoids last-minute inconveniences.
- Some ferry operators offer online reservations, providing added convenience for tourists planning their island-hopping itinerary.

Comfort and Safety:

- Pack essentials such as sunscreen, a hat, and reusable water bottles for a comfortable journey.
- Follow safety guidelines provided by ferry operators. Be aware of life jacket locations and emergency procedures.

Local Insight:

- Strike up conversations with locals and fellow travelers during your ferry journey. They often share invaluable insights into lesser-known attractions, cultural practices, and the best spots for underwater exploration.

Weather Considerations:

- Keep an eye on weather conditions, as sea conditions can vary. Some routes may be affected during adverse weather, so plan accordingly and stay informed.

4.1.5 Walking and Hiking:

Walking and hiking offer a unique perspective, allowing visitors to venture into remote villages, discover hidden waterfalls, and appreciate the lush landscapes that define this South Pacific paradise.

1. Embracing Local Exploration:

- Accessible Attractions: In smaller towns and villages across Vanuatu, walking is an ideal mode of exploration. Many local attractions, cultural sites, and markets are easily accessible on foot, providing an authentic and up-close encounter with the island way of life.

- Cultural Immersion: Walking through local communities allows tourists to engage with the warm and welcoming locals, gaining insights into traditional customs, rituals, and daily routines. It's an opportunity to experience the genuine hospitality that defines Vanuatu.

2. Discovering Scenic Trails and Hiking Routes:

- Nature's Bounty: Vanuatu boasts a diverse topography, and hiking trails abound. From gentle coastal walks to challenging mountain treks, there's a trail for every fitness level and interest.
- Hidden Waterfalls: Hiking unveils hidden gems such as pristine waterfalls tucked away in lush rainforests. The sound of cascading water, coupled with the vibrant flora, creates a serene and picturesque backdrop for unforgettable moments.

3. Responsible Adventure:

- Leave No Trace: As visitors explore on foot, it's essential to adhere to responsible tourism practices. Respect local ecosystems and cultural sites, leaving them undisturbed for future generations to enjoy.
- Guided Tours: To enhance the experience and ensure safety, consider joining guided walking tours led by knowledgeable local guides. These experts provide valuable insights into the flora, fauna, and cultural significance of the areas visited.

4. Practical Considerations:

- Footwear: Comfortable, sturdy footwear is a must for walking and hiking in Vanuatu. Whether navigating village paths or ascending volcanic landscapes, proper shoes provide support and protect against uneven terrain.
- Weather Awareness: Be mindful of weather conditions, especially during the wet season. Trails may become slippery, and river crossings could be more challenging. Plan hikes accordingly and stay informed about local weather forecasts.

5. Must-Visit Walking Destinations:

- Mele Cascades: A popular waterfall hike near Port Vila, offering refreshing pools for a rejuvenating dip.
- Mount Yasur: For the adventurous, hiking up this active volcano on Tanna Island provides a surreal experience with breathtaking views of volcanic activity.
- Millennium Cave Trail: In Espiritu Santo, this challenging but rewarding hike leads through lush landscapes to a stunning cave system.

4.2 Travel Safety Tips

The following travel safety tips are designed to help tourists navigate Vanuatu safely, allowing them to revel in the magic of the South Pacific archipelago responsibly.

1. Respect Local Customs and Traditions:

- Cultural Sensitivity: Familiarize yourself with the local customs and traditions of Vanuatu. This includes understanding appropriate dress codes for specific occasions and respecting sacred sites. Politeness and cultural awareness go a long way in fostering positive interactions with the locals.

2. Stay Informed about Local Conditions:

- Weather Awareness: Vanuatu experiences a tropical climate, and weather conditions can change rapidly. Stay informed about local weather forecasts, especially during the wet season, to plan your activities accordingly and ensure a safe journey.

3. Secure Your Belongings:

- Valuables: Keep your valuables secure, whether exploring urban centers or remote villages. Use a money belt or concealed pouch for important documents and cash, and be vigilant in crowded areas to prevent pickpocketing.

4. Health Precautions:

- Vaccinations: Check with your healthcare provider for recommended vaccinations before traveling to Vanuatu. Ensure you are up-to-date on routine vaccines and any specific vaccinations required for the region.
- Mosquito Protection: Vanuatu is in a region where mosquito-borne diseases are present. Use insect

repellent, wear long sleeves and pants, and consider a bed net to minimize the risk of mosquito-borne illnesses.

5. Transportation Safety:

- Seatbelts and Helmets: When using transportation services, ensure that seatbelts are available and functional. If riding a motorcycle or scooter, always wear a helmet.
- Water Safety: If engaging in water activities, prioritize safety measures such as using life jackets and adhering to guidelines provided by tour operators for snorkeling, diving, or other water-based adventures.

6. Emergency Contacts and Communication:

- Local Emergency Numbers: Save local emergency numbers in your phone, including the contact information of your country's embassy or consulate in Vanuatu.
- Communication Plan: Establish a communication plan with your travel companions, especially if exploring separate areas. Share your whereabouts and have a designated meeting point in case of separation.

7. Responsible Adventure:

- Adventure Tours: If participating in adventure activities such as hiking or water sports, choose reputable tour operators with experienced guides. Follow safety guidelines provided during these activities.

8. Drinking Water and Hydration:

- Safe Water Sources: Ensure the safety of drinking water by consuming bottled or treated water. Hydration is crucial, especially in the tropical climate, so carry a reusable water bottle and refill it from reliable sources.

9. Travel Insurance:

Comprehensive Coverage: Invest in travel insurance that provides comprehensive coverage, including medical emergencies, trip cancellations, and lost belongings. Familiarize yourself with the details of your insurance policy before your trip.

4.3 Travel Insurance and Its Importance

Embarking on a journey to the tropical paradise of Vanuatu is an exciting adventure filled with cultural exploration, stunning landscapes, and vibrant experiences. Amid the anticipation of discovery, one essential aspect that should not be overlooked is securing comprehensive travel insurance. Understanding the importance of travel insurance is not just a matter of practicality; it's a crucial step in ensuring a worry-free and protected travel experience.

1. Emergency Medical Coverage:

- Island Health Services: While Vanuatu provides health services, remote locations may have limited medical facilities. Travel insurance with emergency medical coverage ensures that you have access to medical assistance, evacuation services, and necessary treatment, even in the most secluded areas.

2. Trip Cancellation and Interruption:

- Unforeseen Circumstances: Life is unpredictable, and travel plans can be disrupted by unforeseen events such as illness, family emergencies, or natural disasters. Travel insurance safeguards your investment by covering non-refundable expenses if you need to cancel or cut short your trip.

3. Lost or Delayed Baggage:

- Peace of Mind: Airlines occasionally misplace or delay baggage. Travel insurance provides coverage for lost or delayed baggage, offering reimbursement for essential items you may need during the waiting period.

4. Travel Delays and Missed Connections:

- Flight Disruptions: Travel insurance helps mitigate the impact of unforeseen travel delays or missed connections. It provides coverage for additional expenses, such as accommodation and meals, during unexpected layovers.

5. Evacuation and Repatriation:

- Emergency Situations: In the rare event of a natural disaster, political unrest, or other emergencies, travel insurance ensures that you have access to evacuation services and assistance with repatriation to your home country if necessary.

6. Adventure and Activities Coverage:

- Thrilling Adventures: Vanuatu offers a plethora of adventurous activities, from volcano trekking to water sports. Ensure your travel insurance covers these activities, providing protection in case of accidents or injuries.

7. 24/7 Assistance Services:

- Global Support: Travel insurance typically comes with 24/7 assistance services. Whether you need help with medical emergencies, lost documents, or travel advice, having a reliable support system can make a significant difference in navigating unforeseen challenges.

8. Peace of Mind for You and Your Loved Ones:

- Assurance for Loved Ones: Travel insurance not only safeguards your well-being but also provides peace of mind for your loved ones at home. Knowing that you are covered in case of emergencies allows you to fully immerse yourself in the Vanuatu experience without unnecessary worries.

Before embarking on your journey to Vanuatu, take the time to carefully review and select a travel insurance policy that aligns with your travel plans and preferences. Consider the activities you'll be engaging in, the duration of your stay, and the level of coverage needed.

CHAPTER FIVE

ACCOMMODATION

5.1 Hotels and Resorts

Vanuatu stands as a beacon of luxury with its diverse selection of opulent accommodations. This Pacific paradise caters to the most discerning travelers, offering a spectrum of exquisite hotels and resorts. Whether you seek the vibrant atmosphere of beachfront havens in Port Vila or the tranquil seclusion of retreats on Tanna Island, this section acts as your gateway to a world of sophistication. Delve into detailed insights that illuminate the top-notch facilities, lavish amenities, and impeccable services provided by the crème de la crème of establishments scattered across the archipelago. From panoramic views of azure waters to personalized services, experience the epitome of indulgence in the heart of Vanuatu's breathtaking landscapes.

Recommended Hotels And Resorts With Their Locations

1. Artok Island Retreat

Location: Artok Island

A secluded haven on Artok Island, this retreat offers a unique blend of luxury and tranquility. Surrounded by pristine beaches and lush landscapes, Artok Island Retreat provides an exclusive escape with personalized service.

2. Ratua Island Resort & Spa

Location: Ratua Private Island

A true gem on Ratua Private Island, this eco-lodge boasts overwater villas and rustic chic accommodations. Immerse yourself in nature and enjoy a range of water-based activities in this enchanting corner of Vanuatu.

3. Pele Island Paradise Resort

Location: Pele Island

Nestled on the shores of Pele Island, this resort offers a paradisiacal experience. With beachfront villas and breathtaking views of the Pacific, Pele Island Paradise Resort provides an idyllic retreat away from the hustle and bustle.

4. Port Vila Harbor View Hotel

Location: Port Vila

Overlooking the picturesque Port Vila Harbor, this hotel offers a central and convenient stay in the capital city. Enjoy modern amenities and easy access to Port Vila's vibrant markets, restaurants, and cultural attractions.

5. Ambrym Island Eco Lodge

Location: Ambrym Island

Embrace the natural beauty of Ambrym Island at this eco-friendly lodge. Surrounded by volcanic landscapes and lush greenery, Ambrym Island Eco Lodge provides a unique and sustainable accommodation experience.

6. Vanuatu Grand Resort

Location: Port Vila

A luxurious escape in the heart of Port Vila, Vanuatu Grand Resort offers a range of accommodations with modern amenities. Enjoy the resort's facilities and explore the nearby attractions of the capital city.

7. Ripples on the Bay

Location: Port Vila

This waterfront retreat in Port Vila provides guests with elegantly designed rooms and a personalized atmosphere. Ripples on the Bay offers a serene escape within the lively ambiance of the city.

8. Mystic Sands

Location: Ambrym Island

Mystic Sands on Ambrym Island presents a beachfront paradise. With comfortable accommodations and easy access to the island's natural wonders, it's an ideal retreat for those seeking both relaxation and adventure.

9. Pango Green Motel

Location: Port Vila

Situated in Pango, just outside Port Vila, Pango Green Motel offers budget-friendly accommodations with a focus on sustainability. Experience a comfortable stay while minimizing your environmental footprint.

10. Lapita Beach Resort

Location: Ratua Private Island

Lapita Beach Resort on Ratua Private Island is a luxurious escape featuring exquisite villas and a private beach. Immerse yourself in the serene surroundings and enjoy the resort's world-class amenities for an unforgettable stay.

5.2 Boutique Stays

For discerning travelers yearning for a deeper connection with their surroundings, Vanuatu offers an array of boutique stays that promise an intimate and personalized experience. Discover these hidden gems sprinkled across the archipelago, each a testament to capturing the essence of local culture and hospitality. This dedicated section delves into the distinctive charm of boutique accommodations, unveiling their unique features that set them apart. From thoughtfully curated interiors reflecting indigenous aesthetics to personalized services that cater to individual preferences, every detail is crafted to ensure a harmonious blend of comfort and character. Immerse yourself in the authenticity of Vanuatu through these charming lodgings, where every stay becomes a memorable journey into the heart of Pacific island culture.

Recommended Boutique Stays With Their Locations

1. Village de Santo Resort

Location: Espiritu Santo

Tucked away on the shores of Espiritu Santo, Village de Santo Resort provides an intimate boutique experience. The resort's bungalows showcase local craftsmanship and cultural influences, offering a serene escape with easy access to the island's natural wonders.

2. Aquana Beach Resort

Location: Eratap

Nestled in Eratap, the Aquana Beach Resort is a boutique gem with a focus on sustainable luxury. Embrace the charm of beachfront bungalows surrounded by tropical gardens, and experience personalized service that reflects the warmth of Vanuatu's hospitality.

3. Tanna Tree Top Lodge

Location: Tanna Island

Elevate your stay on Tanna Island at the Tanna Tree Top Lodge, a boutique retreat immersed in the island's lush surroundings. Treehouse-style accommodations offer a unique and immersive experience, allowing guests to connect with nature while enjoying modern comforts.

4. The Havannah, Vanuatu

Location: Efate Island

The Havannah, situated on Efate Island, is a sophisticated boutique stay designed for adult-exclusive tranquility. Luxury villas, each with its own private pool, provide an intimate retreat surrounded by lush landscapes and offering panoramic views of the pristine waters of Havannah Harbour.

5.3 Budget-Friendly Options

Exploring Vanuatu on a budget doesn't mean sacrificing comfort or authenticity. Discover economical yet cozy options, ranging from guesthouses to budget-friendly resorts. This section provides practical tips on where to find affordable accommodation without compromising your Vanuatu experience.

Recommended Budget-Friendly With Their Locations

1. Traveller's Budget Motel

Location: Port Vila

Positioned in the heart of Port Vila, Traveller's Budget Motel offers affordable and cozy guesthouse accommodations. Embrace the city's vibrant atmosphere while enjoying the convenience of budget-friendly lodgings.

2. Blue Pango Motel

Location: Port Vila

Blue Pango Motel provides a comfortable and welcoming guesthouse experience in Port Vila. Close to popular attractions, this budget-friendly option is ideal for travelers seeking a central location without compromising on quality.

3. Tropicana Lagoon Apartments

Location: Port Vila

Situated on the lagoon, Tropicana Lagoon Apartments offers hostel-style accommodations with a laid-back atmosphere.

Enjoy the waterfront views and easy access to the city's activities and attractions.

4. Vila Rose Hotel

Location: Port Vila

Vila Rose Hotel combines affordability with a central location in Port Vila. This guesthouse accommodation provides a convenient base for exploring the city's markets, restaurants, and cultural sites.

5. Namba 2 Backpackers

Location: Port Vila

Catering specifically to budget-conscious travelers, Namba 2 Backpackers offers hostel accommodations with a lively and social atmosphere. Experience Vanuatu's capital city while staying within reach of fellow adventurers.

5.4 Unique Accommodation Experiences

For the adventurous souls seeking something out of the ordinary, Vanuatu offers a variety of unique accommodation experiences. Stay in treehouses overlooking lush landscapes, traditional bungalows nestled in the heart of local communities, or eco-friendly resorts committed to sustainability. Learn about these distinctive options for an unforgettable stay.

Recommended Unique Accommodation With Their Locations

1. Vanuatu Tree House Bungalows

Discover a haven of tranquility and charm at the Tree House Bungalows on Efate Island. Nestled amid the verdant treetops, these unique accommodations offer a perfect blend of traditional Vanuatu architecture and modern comfort. Embrace the enchantment of your secluded setting, where the rustling leaves and birdsong create a natural symphony.

As you ascend to your elevated abode, you'll find that each bungalow is a testament to authenticity, with traditional craftsmanship evident in every detail. From the handcrafted wooden furnishings to the woven palm leaf roofing, the Tree House Bungalows immerse you in the cultural richness of Vanuatu. The interiors are designed for comfort, featuring cozy furnishings and panoramic windows that frame the lush surroundings.

The elevated vantage point not only provides privacy but also offers breathtaking views of the surrounding landscape. Witness the sunrise as it paints the sky in hues of orange and pink, or unwind on your private balcony as the sun sets behind the swaying palm trees. Here, the connection to nature is immediate and rejuvenating.

2. Ratua Private Island - Overwater Villas

For an unparalleled experience of luxury, escape to Ratua Private Island on Ratua Island. Indulge in the epitome of overwater living, where rustic charm seamlessly intertwines with modern amenities to create a truly exclusive retreat.

The overwater villas at Ratua Private Island redcfine the concept of indulgence, providing an unforgettable and intimate stay surrounded by the crystal-clear waters of the Pacific.

Step onto the wooden deck of your villa and feel the gentle lapping of the waves beneath. Each villa is a masterpiece of design, featuring traditional thatched roofing, elegant wooden interiors, and open spaces that invite the natural beauty of the island indoors. The clear floor panels allow you to witness the vibrant marine life swimming beneath your feet.

Ratua Private Island doesn't just offer accommodation; it crafts an entire experience. From personalized butler service to private plunge pools overlooking the ocean, every aspect of your stay is tailored to create moments of indulgence and relaxation. This is a haven where luxury meets the untouched beauty of Vanuatu.

3. Tamanu on the Beach - Eco-Friendly Bungalows

Journey to Aore Island and uncover eco-friendly luxury at Tamanu on the Beach. This boutique resort redefines sustainable design, offering a collection of unique bungalows that blend seamlessly with the natural beauty of the beach and tropical landscapes. From the moment you arrive, you'll sense the commitment to both luxury and environmental consciousness.

The eco-friendly bungalows at Tamanu on the Beach are architectural gems, constructed with locally sourced materials that reflect Vanuatu's dedication to preserving its pristine surroundings. Solar power, rainwater harvesting, and other eco friendly initiatives are seamlessly integrated into the design, ensuring that your stay leaves minimal impact on the environment.

Each bungalow is a sanctuary of comfort and style, with spacious interiors, private verandas, and panoramic views of the azure waters. Whether you're lounging on the beach or exploring the nearby coral reefs, Tamanu on the Beach invites you to experience the beauty of Vanuatu with a sustainable touch.

4. Lonnoc Beach Bungalows - Beachfront Treehouses

In the heart of Espiritu Santo, Lonnoc Beach Bungalows beckons with an extraordinary stay in beachfront treehouses. As you step onto the sandy shores, you'll discover a unique and intimate retreat where the sound of waves becomes your soundtrack, and stunning ocean views define your stay.

Perched amidst the lush vegetation, these beachfront treehouses offer an immersive experience in nature without compromising on comfort. The interiors are designed to evoke a sense of island living, with wooden furnishings, open-air spaces, and canopied beds that create an ambiance of tropical elegance.

Waking up in the morning, you'll find yourself surrounded by the natural beauty of Espiritu Santo. Enjoy a leisurely breakfast on your private balcony as you take in panoramic views of the pristine beach. Lonnoc Beach Bungalows provides an idyllic setting where the simplicity of beachfront living is elevated to an art form.

5. Village de Santo Resort - Canopy Villas

Immerse yourself in the captivating beauty of Espiritu Santo at Village de Santo Resort, where canopy villas offer a unique treetop experience. Surrounded by lush vegetation, these accommodations provide a perfect blend of seclusion and luxury. The resort's commitment to creating an intimate and serene atmosphere is evident in every detail of the canopy villas.

As you ascend to your elevated haven, you'll find yourself in a world of tranquility. The canopy villas are designed with a harmonious balance of modern comfort and traditional elegance, featuring spacious interiors, private balconies, and large windows that invite the natural light and scenery indoors.

The lush vegetation surrounding the canopy villas adds to the sense of seclusion, creating a tranquil sanctuary where you can unwind and connect with nature. Village de Santo Resort invites you to experience the best of both worlds – the enchantment of treetop living and the luxury of a refined retreat.

5.5 Booking Accommodation in Advance

For tourists planning a visit to Vanuatu, booking accommodation in advance is a strategic and advisable step to ensure a seamless and enjoyable travel experience. Vanuatu, with its diverse array of islands and attractions, attracts visitors seeking everything from luxurious resorts to intimate guesthouses, and unique boutique stays. Here's why booking accommodation in advance is highly recommended:

1. Ensures Availability:

Vanuatu, despite its pristine beauty and laid-back atmosphere, is becoming an increasingly popular tourist destination. By booking your accommodation in advance, you secure your spot in your preferred lodging, especially during peak travel seasons.

2. Diverse Options:

Vanuatu offers a range of accommodations to suit every traveler's preferences. Whether you're looking for overwater bungalows, beachfront resorts, boutique stays, or budget-friendly guesthouses, the islands cater to various tastes. Booking in advance allows you to choose from a diverse range of options based on your budget and preferences.

3. Optimal Planning:

Planning your accommodation in advance allows you to organize your itinerary efficiently. Knowing where you'll be staying allows you to plan your daily activities and sightseeing with ease, optimizing your time on the islands.

4. Special Offers and Discounts:

Many accommodations in Vanuatu offer special deals and discounts for guests who book in advance. By taking advantage of these promotions, you not only secure your stay but may also enjoy cost savings or additional perks, enhancing the overall value of your trip.

5. Peace of Mind:

Traveling to a new destination can sometimes be daunting, especially if you're unsure about where you'll be staying. Booking your accommodation in advance provides a sense of security and peace of mind, allowing you to focus on enjoying your vacation rather than worrying about finding suitable lodgings upon arrival.

6. Customized Experiences:

Some accommodations in Vanuatu offer unique experiences, such as cultural immersion programs, guided tours, or special events. Booking in advance allows you to explore and select accommodations that provide these extra touches, tailoring your stay to be even more memorable and enriching.

7. Logistical Convenience:

Arriving in a new destination can be tiring, and having your accommodation prearranged eliminates the stress of finding a place to stay upon arrival. You can simply relax, knowing that your lodging is ready and waiting for you.

8. Flexibility for Changes:

While planning is crucial, some accommodations offer flexible cancellation policies or modification options. This allows you to make changes to your reservation if needed, providing a degree of flexibility in your travel plans.

5.6 Tips for Finding the Right Lodging for Your Needs

Here are essential tips to help you find accommodations that perfectly align with your needs, ensuring a comfortable and enriching stay:

- Define Your Priorities: Begin by identifying your priorities. Whether it's proximity to attractions, budget constraints, or a specific type of experience, clarifying your priorities will streamline the selection process.
- Consider Location: The islands of Vanuatu offer diverse landscapes, from bustling urban centers to secluded beachfronts. Consider the location that aligns with your interests. If you seek a vibrant atmosphere, opt for accommodations in Port Vila. For a more relaxed and secluded experience, explore options on the outer islands.
- Accommodation Type: Vanuatu boasts a range of accommodations, from luxurious resorts and boutique stays to budget-friendly guesthouses. Choose the type of lodging that resonates with your travel style and preferences.
- Read Reviews: Before making a reservation, read reviews from fellow travelers. Websites like TripAdvisor and booking platforms often feature reviews that provide insights into the quality of service, amenities, and overall guest experience.
- Budget Considerations: Establish a clear budget for accommodation. Vanuatu offers options for various budget ranges, so whether you're looking for a lavish resort or a more economical guesthouse, there's

something for everyone. Be sure to factor in additional costs such as meals and activities.

- Explore Local Options: Consider staying in locally-run accommodations for a more authentic experience. Guesthouses and smaller resorts often offer a personal touch, allowing you to connect with the local culture and community.
- Check for Amenities: Depending on your preferences, amenities can significantly impact your stay. If you value relaxation, seek accommodations with spa facilities. For families, consider resorts with kid-friendly amenities. Wi-Fi, air conditioning, and on-site dining are also factors to consider.
- Booking in Advance: Especially during peak seasons, it's advisable to book your accommodation in advance. This not only secures your preferred lodging but also helps in securing the best rates.
- Flexible Cancellation Policies: Given the uncertainties of travel, opt for accommodations with flexible cancellation policies. This provides peace of mind in case your plans need to be adjusted.
- Connect with Locals: If you're seeking an immersive experience, consider accommodations that facilitate interaction with locals. Homestays, community-based tourism, and smaller lodgings often provide a more intimate connection to the destination.

By carefully considering these tips, you can ensure that your choice of lodging enhances your overall Vanuatu experience, offering comfort, convenience, and a genuine connection to the beauty of the South Pacific.

CHAPTER SIX

DINING IN VANUATU

6.1 Must-Taste Dishes and Local Delicacies

1. Lap Lap:

Description: Lap Lap is a traditional Vanuatu dish that epitomizes the fusion of local flavors. It typically consists of grated root vegetables, such as yams or taro, mixed with coconut cream and a choice of meat or seafood. The mixture is then wrapped in banana leaves and baked to perfection, creating a delicious and hearty dish.

2. Coconut Crab:

Description: Celebrated as a local delicacy, the Coconut Crab is a unique culinary experience in Vanuatu. Known for its sweet and succulent meat, this large land crab is often prepared in various ways, including grilling or baking. Its rich flavor and cultural significance make it a must-try for seafood enthusiasts.

3. Vanuatu Bougna:

Description: Bougna is a communal feast that brings people together to celebrate local traditions. This dish features a combination of meats, such as chicken, pork, or fish, mixed with root vegetables and coconut milk. The ingredients are wrapped in banana leaves and cooked in an earth oven, resulting in a flavorful and aromatic culinary delight.

4. Nanggaria:

Description: Nanggaria is a popular dessert in Vanuatu, showcasing the sweetness of coconut milk. This chilled pudding is often flavored with tropical fruits, providing a refreshing and delightful way to end a meal. Its creamy texture and tropical notes make it a favorite among those with a sweet tooth.

5. Vanuatu Taro Cake:

Description: Taro, a staple root vegetable in Vanuatu, takes center stage in this unique dish. The Vanuatu Taro Cake is a savory delight made from grated taro, coconut cream, and sometimes a touch of local spices. It is baked or steamed to perfection, resulting in a moist and flavorful cake with a hint of sweetness from the coconut.

6. Poulet Fish:

Description: Poulet Fish, also known as Chicken Fish, is a popular seafood dish in Vanuatu. It typically features a fish fillet marinated in a flavorful blend of local herbs and spices, giving it a distinct taste. Grilled or fried to perfection, Poulet Fish offers a delicious and aromatic experience that highlights the freshness of Vanuatu's seafood.

7. Vanuatu Fruit Salad with Coconut Dressing:

Description: Enjoy the vibrant tropical fruits of Vanuatu in a refreshing fruit salad with coconut dressing. This light and healthy dessert showcase a medley of fresh fruits, such as pineapple, papaya, and banana, drizzled with a coconut milk dressing. It's a perfect way to indulge in the natural sweetness of the Pacific islands.

6.2 International Flavors

The archipelago, nestled in the South Pacific, not only boasts a rich tapestry of indigenous tastes but also embraces global culinary influences, making it a paradise for discerning food enthusiasts.

French Influence:

The lingering influence of Vanuatu's colonial history is evident in its culinary scene, particularly through the presence of French-inspired bakeries and cafes. As you meander through the charming streets, the aroma of freshly baked pastries and bread wafts through the air, inviting you to indulge in a culinary journey with a touch of French elegance. Whether you're sipping on a perfectly brewed coffee or savoring a flaky croissant, these establishments pay homage to the country's colonial past while offering a delightful fusion of local and French flavors.

Asian Fusion:

Venture beyond the traditional and dive into the world of Asian-inspired dishes that showcase a seamless fusion of local ingredients with exotic flavors. Select restaurants across the islands have mastered the art of blending Asian culinary techniques with Vanuatu's fresh produce, resulting in a menu that surprises and delights. From tantalizing stir-fries to delectable sushi creations, the Asian influence adds a dynamic and creative dimension to Vanuatu's gastronomic offerings.

International Dining Hubs:

For those with a more eclectic palate, Vanuatu harbors dining establishments that cater to a global audience. These hubs present a diverse menu that spans continents, offering everything from Mediterranean-inspired dishes to the bold and vibrant flavors of South American cuisine. Whether you crave the robust spices of Mexican fare or the subtle sophistication of Italian cooking, these international dining spots provide a taste of the world within the enchanting backdrop of Vanuatu.

In essence, Vanuatu's culinary scene is a testament to its openness to the global flavors that have found a home on its shores. The juxtaposition of local traditions with international influences creates a harmonious symphony of tastes, inviting you to embark on a gastronomic adventure that transcends geographical boundaries. So, as you explore the islands, be prepared to savor not only the authentic local dishes but also the delightful surprises that await in the form of French-inspired delicacies, Asian-infused creations, and a global menu that reflects Vanuatu's welcoming and diverse spirit.

6.3 Local Market Adventures

Immerse yourself in the vibrant atmosphere of Vanuatu's local markets, where an array of fresh produce, seafood, and handcrafted goods await. Navigate through bustling stalls, interact with local vendors, and sample the diverse array of ingredients that make up Vanuatu's culinary tapestry.

Port Vila Central Market:

Nestled in the heart of Vanuatu's capital, Port Vila Central Market beckons visitors to immerse themselves in a vibrant and bustling kaleidoscope of sights, sounds, and scents. This lively market is a sensory haven, where the vibrant colors of fresh fruits and vegetables compete for attention, and the air is filled with the enticing aroma of exotic spices. As you navigate through the market's lively stalls, you'll encounter a treasure trove of locally grown produce, from juicy tropical fruits to crisp, garden-fresh vegetables. The market isn't just a feast for the senses—it's a cultural experience, providing a glimpse into the daily lives of the friendly locals who gather here to sell their goods. Handmade crafts, woven baskets, and traditional artifacts add to the eclectic mix, making Port Vila Central Market a must-visit destination for those seeking an authentic taste of Vanuatu's daily life and culinary delights.

Luganville Market:

Venture to Luganville, where the market scene unfolds as a vibrant and dynamic display of local life. Luganville Market is a bustling hub known for its lively atmosphere and an impressive array of locally sourced products. Stroll through the market's diverse sections, each offering a unique glimpse into the region's rich agricultural abundance. From the freshest fruits and vegetables to aromatic spices and herbs, Luganville Market is a sensory adventure that captures the essence of Vanuatu's agricultural prowess. Engage with friendly vendors who are eager to share stories about their produce and local traditions. The market's energy is infectious, and the variety of goods on display reflects the island's commitment to sustainable living and traditional practices. Whether you're seeking fresh ingredients for a home-cooked meal or unique souvenirs to commemorate your visit, Luganville Market promises an authentic and immersive experience in the heart of Vanuatu's second-largest town.

6.4 Dining Etiquette

Embarking on a culinary journey through Vanuatu goes beyond just savoring delicious dishes—it involves immersing yourself in the cultural nuances of dining. To fully appreciate the local experience, it's essential to navigate Vanuatu's dining culture with respect, understanding, and an openness to traditions that have been passed down through generations.

In Vanuatu, communal meals hold profound significance. These gatherings are not just about sharing food but also about fostering a sense of community and unity. To engage respectfully in communal meals, visitors are encouraged to participate with an open heart. Accepting invitations to share a meal with locals provides an intimate glimpse into their way of life, where generosity and inclusivity are highly valued.

Traditional ceremonies often accompany meals in Vanuatu, adding layers of meaning to the dining experience. From the preparation of food to the sharing of stories, each element holds cultural significance. Taking the time to understand these rituals enhances your connection to the local culture, allowing you to partake in the rich tapestry of Vanuatu's traditions.

Hospitality is a cornerstone of Vanuatu's culture, and this warmth is evident in the way meals are shared. Locals take pride in offering the best of what their land and sea have to offer, showcasing the abundance of fresh, locally sourced ingredients. Expressing gratitude for these offerings is not only polite but also a way to acknowledge the effort and care that goes into preparing each dish.

As you dine in Vanuatu, embrace the opportunity to learn from the locals. Engage in conversations, ask questions, and be open to the stories they share about their culinary heritage. By approaching dining with cultural sensitivity, you not only enrich your own experience but also contribute to the preservation and appreciation of Vanuatu's unique and vibrant traditions. So, let each meal become a gateway to understanding, connection, and the celebration of the rich tapestry that defines Vanuatu's dining culture.

6.5 Recommended Restaurants with Their Locations

Discover a curated list of recommended restaurants, each offering a unique culinary experience in various locations across Vanuatu. From beachside cafes to upscale dining establishments, these venues promise a delightful journey for your taste buds.

1. The Beach Bar & Grill (Port Vila):

Location: Erakor Lagoon, Port Vila

Description: Indulge in a beachfront dining experience at The Beach Bar & Grill. With a menu inspired by local ingredients and international culinary trends, this restaurant offers a relaxed atmosphcre wlth stunning views of Erakor Lagoon.

2. Tamanu on the Beach (Efate):

Location: White Sands Road, Efate

Description: Nestled on the shores of Efate, Tamanu on the Beach provides a tranquil beachfront setting. Known for its fusion of local and international flavors, this restaurant offers a sophisticated dining experience with a focus on fresh, seasonal ingredients.

3. Chill Restaurant & Bar (Tanna):

Location: Lowelkas Cove, Tanna

Description: Located in the picturesque Lowelkas Cove, Chill Restaurant & Bar on Tanna Island provides a relaxed atmosphere. Guests can unwind while savoring a blend of Vanuatu and international dishes, creating a perfect island dining experience.

4. Deco Stop Lodge Restaurant (Espiritu Santo):

Location: Lonnoc Beach, Espiritu Santo

Description: Experience island dining at its finest at Deco Stop Lodge Restaurant. With a focus on fresh seafood and locally sourced produce, this restaurant on Espiritu Santo offers a taste of the Pacific in a laid-back, beachside setting.

5. Le Marché Restaurant (Port Vila):

Location: Lini Highway, Port Vila

Description: Discover a culinary gem at Le Marché Restaurant in Port Vila. This establishment combines French and Pacific flavors, offering a diverse menu featuring locally sourced ingredients and a charming, intimate ambiance.

6. Warhorse Saloon (Port Vila):

Location: Rue Dart, Port Vila

Description: For a taste of the American West in the South Pacific, visit Warhorse Saloon. Located in Port Vila, this restaurant serves up hearty dishes, from burgers to steaks, in a Western-inspired atmosphere.

7. L'Houstalet (Port Vila):

Location: Kumul Highway, Port Vila

Description: Embrace the French influence at L'Houstalet in Port Vila. This restaurant offers a menu that reflects the best of French and Vanuatu cuisine, creating a culinary experience that is both refined and welcoming.

8. Tropicana Lagoon Breeze Café (Port Vila):

Location: Elluk, Port Vila

Description: Situated in Elluk, Tropicana Lagoon Breeze Café provides a relaxed and tropical setting. The menu features a mix of international and local dishes, and guests can enjoy the serene lagoon views while savoring their meals.

CHAPTER SEVEN

ENTERTAINMENT AND NIGHTLIFE

7.1 Nightclubs and Lounges with their Locations

7.1.1 Club Tropicana: A Night of Energetic Revelry in the Heart of Port Vila

Located in the bustling heart of Port Vila on Efate Island, Club Tropicana stands as a beacon of lively nightlife, beckoning locals and tourists alike to experience the vibrant energy it exudes. The neon lights and pulsating beats draw you into an atmosphere of pure excitement and celebration. This lively nightclub is a testament to Port Vila's dynamic nightlife scene, and Club Tropicana, with its prime location, takes the lead in delivering an unforgettable experience.

As you step into Club Tropicana, the rhythmic thump of the latest beats sets the tone for the night ahead. The dance floor, bathed in neon lights, becomes a canvas for patrons to express themselves through dance and revelry. The club's diverse music selection ensures that there's something for everyone, from chart-topping international hits to local tunes that capture the essence of Vanuatu's rich musical heritage.

Beyond the dance floor, Club Tropicana offers a haven for those seeking a more relaxed ambiance. The stylish lounge setting provides a comfortable space to unwind with friends or meet new ones. The skilled bartenders craft signature cocktails that tantalize the taste buds, offering a delightful complement to the pulsating beats in the background. Whether you're a dance enthusiast or a connoisseur of crafted cocktails, Club Tropicana caters to every facet of your nightlife desires.

7.1.2 Volcano Vibes Lounge: Where Relaxation Meets Excitement on Tanna Island

On the enchanting Tanna Island, Volcano Vibes Lounge presents a different but equally captivating nightlife experience. This unique lounge stands as a testament to the island's laid-back charm, providing an ideal setting for those seeking a more relaxed yet exciting evening. Nestled in a tropical paradise, Volcano Vibes Lounge invites patrons to enjoy the soothing sounds of local music, sip on refreshing tropical drinks, and share travel tales with fellow adventurers.

The lounge's atmosphere is infused with the spirit of Tanna, creating an intimate space where the natural beauty of the island converges with the cultural richness of its people. Live performances by local artists add a personal touch to the experience, showcasing the vibrant artistic talent that thrives in this corner of Vanuatu. For those looking to unwind in a more tranquil setting, Volcano Vibes Lounge on Tanna Island provides the perfect escape.

7.1.3 Harbor Lights Club: Dancing Beneath the Stars in Luganville, Espiritu Santo

Luganville, situated on the picturesque Espiritu Santo, hosts the ever-inviting Harbor Lights Club. This waterfront venue provides a stunning backdrop for a night of dancing and socializing. As you step into the club, the view of the harbor unfolds before you, creating a captivating ambiance that seamlessly blends the natural beauty of Espiritu Santo with the rhythmic beats of the night.

Harbor Lights Club offers a diverse musical journey, mixing international hits with local rhythms. The fusion of cultural influences in the music creates an inviting atmosphere that caters to both the global traveler and those seeking a taste of local Espiritu Santo vibes. Whether you're sipping a cocktail on the outdoor terrace or dancing beneath the stars, Harbor Lights Club ensures a night of unforgettable moments in this tropical haven.

7.1.4 Mystique Lounge: Discovering Intimacy and Sophistication in Port Olry, Espiritu Santo

In the charming town of Port Olry on Espiritu Santo, Mystique Lounge unveils itself as a hidden gem, inviting patrons to a night of intimacy and sophistication. This lounge, tucked away from the hustle and bustle, offers a serene escape for those seeking a more refined evening. The ambiance is one of understated elegance, with comfortable seating arrangements and a selection of fine wines that beckon those with a discerning palate.

Mystique Lounge stands out as a venue where live performances take center stage, adding an extra layer of sophistication to the night. The occasional themed events further elevate the experience, providing a touch of novelty to each visit. Whether you're enjoying a quiet conversation with friends or immersing yourself in the live entertainment, Mystique Lounge in Port Olry promises an enchanting night in a setting that marries elegance with the charm of Espiritu Santo's coastal beauty.

7.2 Family-Friendly Entertainment

Vanuatu is not only a paradise for adults but also an ideal destination for family adventures. Find entertainment suitable for all ages.

7.2.1 Kid-Friendly Activities: A World of Adventure for the Little Ones

Vanuatu welcomes families with open arms, offering a plethora of exciting and educational activities tailored for children. Whether you're seeking outdoor adventures, interactive museums, or family-friendly resorts, the islands provide a diverse array of experiences that will captivate the imagination of the little ones.

Exciting and Educational Experiences:

Vanuatu is a playground for young adventurers. Engage your children in thrilling outdoor activities such as snorkeling in crystal-clear waters, exploring vibrant coral reefs, or embarking on nature trails that lead to hidden waterfalls. The islands' natural beauty serves as an expansive classroom where children can learn about marine life, ecosystems, and the importance of preserving the environment.

Parks, Museums, and Interactive Attractions:

For a day of family fun, explore the parks, museums, and interactive attractions scattered across Vanuatu. Port Vila, on Efate Island, boasts charming parks where children can play and parents can relax amidst tropical landscapes. Discover interactive museums offering hands-on exhibits, allowing young minds to delve into the history, culture, and biodiversity of the islands.

Family-Friendly Resorts with Amenities for Children:

Vanuatu's family-friendly resorts go the extra mile to ensure a comfortable and enjoyable stay for families. From dedicated kids' clubs with engaging activities to child-friendly pools and play areas, these resorts cater to the needs of both parents and children. The warm hospitality of the locals extends to the youngest members of your family, creating a welcoming and inclusive atmosphere.

7.2.2 Cultural Experiences for the Whole Family: Journeying into Vanuatu's Rich Heritage

Vanuatu's cultural tapestry is woven with traditions, stories, and vibrant performances that families can enjoy together. Immerse yourselves in the heart of local customs through a variety of cultural experiences that are both entertaining and enlightening.

Explore Cultural Events Together:

Vanuatu hosts a calendar of cultural events that provide a window into the islanders' way of life. Joining these festivities allows families to witness traditional dances, music performances, and rituals that have been passed down through generations. From lively celebrations to more intimate gatherings, these events offer a unique insight into the spirit of Vanuatu.

Traditional Performances, Storytelling, and Local Crafts:

Enrich your family's experience by attending traditional performances that showcase the vibrant heritage of Vanuatu. Storytelling sessions narrate the legends and myths that form the foundation of the islanders' cultural identity. Engage in hands-on experiences with local crafts, where children can create their own souvenirs, fostering a connection with the artistic traditions of the islands.

Family-Oriented Tours:

Embark on family-oriented tours designed to bring the rich history of Vanuatu to life. Explore archaeological sites, visit ancient villages, and witness the art of traditional craftsmanship. Knowledgeable guides share stories that captivate young minds, creating an educational and immersive experience that allows families to connect with the roots of Vanuatu's diverse communities.

In Vanuatu, the concept of family extends beyond blood relations, and the islands offer a tapestry of experiences that ensure every member, regardless of age, is an integral part of the adventure. From thrilling outdoor pursuits for the little adventurers to cultural explorations that resonate with the whole family, Vanuatu invites you to create lasting memories in a setting where the warmth of the people matches the beauty of the landscape.

7.3 Special Events and Festivals

While specific dates for some festivals may vary from year to year, the following is an overview of some major special events and festivals in Vanuatu along with general months during which they typically occur. It's advisable to check local sources or tourism offices for exact dates when you want to visit:

1. Pentecost Land Dive: Plunging into Tradition on Pentecost Island

Location: Pentecost Island

Month: April

Every April, Pentecost Island comes alive with the thrilling and symbolic Pentecost Land Dive, a tradition that is both a rite of passage and a jubilant celebration of the yam harvest. As a spectator, you'll find yourself at the heart of a mesmerizing spectacle as locals, adorned in traditional attire, climb tall wooden towers. With nothing but vines tied to their ankles, they dive headfirst towards the earth below. This ancient and daring ritual is believed to ensure a bountiful yam harvest, making it a vital cultural practice for the people of Pentecost. As a visitor, witnessing the Land Dive offers a profound glimpse into the island's cultural legacy, showcasing the courage, spirituality, and connection to the land that define this extraordinary tradition.

2. John Frum Cargo Cult Celebrations: Mystical Revelry on Tanna Island

Location: Tanna Island

Month: February

In February, Tanna Island becomes a captivating stage for the John Frum Cargo Cult Celebrations. This mystical event revolves around the John Frum cult, a belief system associated with a messianic figure tied to cargo cults. The islanders celebrate with traditional dances, mesmerizing rituals, and communal feasts that transport you into a world of spiritual fervor. Embracing the John Frum Cargo Cult Celebrations is an invitation to witness the intertwining of belief, tradition, and community spirit on Tanna, offering a unique and immersive experience that lingers in the memory long after the festivities conclude.

3. Port Vila Arts and Music Festival: A Tapestry of Creativity on Efate Island

Location: Port Vila, Efate Island

Month: July

Come July, Port Vila on Efate Island transforms into a vibrant canvas of creativity during the Port Vila Arts and Music Festival. This lively event showcases the dynamic artistic spirit of Vanuatu, featuring a diverse array of local and international artists. Immerse yourself in the rhythms of live music, be enchanted by traditional performances, explore art exhibitions, and indulge in culinary delights that reflect the rich cultural diversity of the islands. The Port Vila

Arts and Music Festival is a celebration of Vanuatu's creative soul, inviting visitors to engage with the artistic heartbeat of the archipelago in a lively and communal atmosphere.

4. Independence Day Celebrations: A Nationwide Jubilation

Location: Nationwide

Date: July 30th

On July 30th, Vanuatu unites in a nationwide celebration to mark Independence Day, commemorating the momentous occasion when the archipelago gained freedom from joint British and French colonial rule in 1980. Independence Day becomes a testament to the resilience and spirit of the nation, celebrated with exuberant parades, cultural displays, and patriotic events that resonate across the islands. As a visitor, joining in the festivities allows you to witness the pride and unity of the people of Vanuatu, offering a firsthand experience of the joyous atmosphere that accompanies this significant day in the nation's history.

5. Naghol Land Diving Festival: Leaping into Tradition on Pentecost Island

Location: Pentecost Island

Month: April to June (exact date varies)

The Naghol Land Diving Festival, spanning from April to June (with the exact date varying annually), is a captivating spectacle on Pentecost Island. Rooted in ancient fertility rites, this daring tradition involves men leaping from wooden towers with vines tied to their ankles. The festival marks the yam harvest season, and the dives are believed to ensure a bountiful crop. As a spectator, you become part of the cultural narrative, witnessing this ancient practice that holds profound significance for the people of Pentecost. The Naghol Land Diving Festival is a unique opportunity to connect with Vanuatu's cultural heritage and witness the courage and spirituality embedded in this age-old ritual.

6. Rom Dance Festival: Unveiling Mystical Traditions on Ambrym Island

Location: Ambrym Island

Month: September

In September, Ambrym Island hosts the Rom Dance Festival, a captivating celebration that unveils the island's mystical traditions. The festival features traditional dances, intricate rituals, and the mesmerizing display of masks. Ambrym's unique cultural identity comes to life through the vibrant performances and symbolic expressions showcased during the festival. As a visitor, the Rom Dance Festival provides a rare opportunity to witness the island's spiritual richness, offering a deeper understanding of the customs and beliefs that have shaped Ambrym's cultural landscape. The festival is a visual and sensory journey into the heart of Ambrym's traditions, leaving a lasting imprint on those fortunate enough to witness this captivating celebration.

7. Water Music Festival: Harmonizing with Nature on Gaua Island

Location: Gaua Island

Month: August

In the tranquil embrace of Gaua Island, the Water Music Festival in August is a unique celebration that harmonizes with the island's natural surroundings. Experience the mesmerizing sounds of water music as local performers create rhythmic melodies by skillfully hitting the water's surface. This extraordinary auditory experience is a testament to the cultural heritage of Gaua and its deep connection to water-based traditions. The festival not only captivates the senses but also provides insight into the island's spiritual relationship with its natural environment. Attendees become part of a sensory journey, where the elemental sounds of water serve as a backdrop to a celebration of Gaua's rich cultural legacy.

8. Back to My Roots Festival: Tanna Island's Cultural Odyssey in October

Location: Tanna Island

Month: October

Tanna Island comes alive in October with the Back to My Roots Festival, a jubilant celebration of the island's diverse cultural heritage. The festival is a tapestry of traditional dances, captivating storytelling, and vibrant cultural exhibitions. As a visitor, you're invited to join in the festivities and witness the preservation and showcasing of Tanna's customs and traditions. The Back to My Roots Festival is not only a joyous occasion but also a significant effort to ensure the continuity of Tanna's cultural legacy. It provides an immersive experience, allowing attendees to connect with the island's roots, forging lasting memories and a deeper appreciation for Tanna's cultural richness.

CHAPTER EIGHT

CULTURAL EXPERIENCES

8.1 Museums and Galleries

One of the most captivating ways to delve into the soul of this nation is through its museums and galleries, which serve as windows into the rich history and heritage of the Ni-Vanuatu people.

Vanuatu's Cultural Heritage Unveiled

A visit to Vanuatu's museums and galleries promises an immersive journey through time, allowing travelers to unravel the intricacies of the nation's past. The artifacts housed within these cultural institutions tell tales of resilience, traditions, and the unique evolution of Vanuatu's diverse communities.

Exploring Artifacts and Historical Exhibits

Step into the meticulously curated spaces of these cultural havens, and you'll find a treasure trove of artifacts that narrate the story of Vanuatu's indigenous cultures. Traditional tools, ceremonial objects, and ancient relics provide a tangible connection to the customs and practices that have shaped the Ni-Vanuatu way of life for centuries.

Venture beyond the surface, and historical exhibits within these venues unfold the narrative of Vanuatu's encounters with colonial powers, its struggles for independence, and the subsequent forging of a national identity. The juxtaposition of ancient artifacts and more recent historical exhibits creates a dynamic and comprehensive overview of Vanuatu's cultural continuum.

The Vanuatu Cultural Centre: A Cultural Epicenter in Port Vila

Among the noteworthy venues is the Vanuatu Cultural Centre, located in the capital city of Port Vila. This cultural epicenter stands as a testament to the preservation and celebration of Vanuatu's heritage. As you step into the center, you are greeted by captivating displays of traditional art and artifacts that reflect the essence of Ni-Vanuatu creativity and craftsmanship.

The Vanuatu Cultural Centre serves as a hub for the promotion of local artistry and the safeguarding of intangible cultural heritage. Its exhibits showcase a kaleidoscope of artifacts, from intricately woven mats to elaborately carved ceremonial masks, each carrying profound cultural significance. The center's commitment to education and cultural awareness is evident in its efforts to engage visitors with interactive displays and interpretive materials, providing context to the exhibited items.

A Journey through Diverse Communities

What makes the exploration of these cultural repositories truly enriching is the diversity of the communities they represent. Vanuatu comprises over 80 islands, each with its own distinct cultural practices and traditions. Museums and galleries become gateways to understanding the nuanced differences and shared threads that weave together the fabric of Vanuatu's collective identity.

As you traverse these cultural spaces, you'll encounter the unique artistry of the people from Pentecost with their awe-inspiring land diving rituals, or the mesmerizing sand drawings of Ambrym. The diversity in artistic expression reflects the deep-rooted connection between the Ni-Vanuatu and their natural surroundings, offering a profound appreciation for the symbiotic relationship between culture and environment.

In essence, the museums and galleries of Vanuatu serve not only as repositories of artifacts but as living testimonies to the resilience, creativity, and cultural wealth of its people. They provide a bridge between the past and present, inviting visitors to engage with the traditions that continue to shape Vanuatu's evolving narrative.

8.2 Cultural Arts and Heritage

Vanuatu, a jewel in the Pacific, invites you to embark on a sensory journey, immersing yourself in the vibrant cultural arts and heritage that define this archipelago. Here, tradition is not just a relic of the past but a living, breathing entity passed down through generations, manifesting in mesmerizing ways that captivate the spirit and ignite the imagination.

The Rhythm of Tradition: Dance, Music, and Storytelling

In the heart of Vanuatu's cultural landscape lies the rhythmic pulse of traditional dance, an art form that transcends time and weaves tales of ancestral stories and spiritual connections. Indigenous dance performances, adorned with elaborate costumes and accompanied by pulsating beats, provide a visual and auditory feast that immerses spectators in the very essence of Ni-Vanuatu identity.

As you witness these dances, each movement tells a story – a narrative etched in the collective memory of the community. The swaying hips, rhythmic stomping, and intricate hand movements are a language that speaks of ancient rituals, social dynamics, and the profound relationship between the people and the land. It's a visceral experience that transcends mere entertainment, offering a profound insight into the cultural ethos of Vanuatu.

Accompanying the dance is the symphony of traditional music, where beats resonate with the heartbeat of the islands. Instruments like the slit gong, bamboo pipes, and conch shells create a melodic fusion that is both haunting and uplifting. The music serves not only as an accompaniment to dance but as a storytelling medium, preserving narratives that might otherwise be lost to the sands of time.

Adding another layer to this cultural tapestry is the art of storytelling, an ancient tradition where oral histories are passed down from elders to the younger generation. Griots and storytellers weave narratives that delve into the very fabric of Ni-Vanuatu life – tales of creation, heroes, and the challenges faced by their ancestors. These stories, often accompanied by music and dance, serve as a living library, connecting the present to a rich past.

Local Festivals and Ceremonies: The Living Traditions

To truly immerse yourself in the cultural heartbeat of Vanuatu, attending local festivals and ceremonies is a must. These events provide a front-row seat to the living traditions of the Ni-Vanuatu people, where ancient customs come alive, and communities unite in celebration.

Whether it's the exhilarating Naghol (land diving) ceremony on Pentecost, where daring individuals take a leap with only vines tied to their ankles, or the colorful celebrations of Independence Day, each festival is a window into the soul of Vanuatu. Participate in the festivities, taste traditional foods, and engage with locals as they proudly showcase their customs.

These gatherings are not merely performances for visitors; they are integral to the social fabric of Vanuatu, fostering a sense of community and shared identity. Attending these events goes beyond being a spectator; it is an opportunity to become a participant in the living culture of the islands.

A Deeper Appreciation for Vanuatu's Cultural Tapestry

As you immerse yourself in the dance, music, and storytelling that echo through the islands, a deeper appreciation for Vanuatu's cultural tapestry begins to unfold. It's a tapestry woven with threads of resilience, creativity, and a profound connection to the land and sea. The enchantment lies not only in the performances themselves but in the realization that these traditions are not staged for the benefit of tourists but are authentic expressions of identity and community.

In the next section of this guide, we will delve into understanding local customs and traditions, providing insights into the daily practices, social norms, and cultural etiquettes that will enhance your cultural journey through Vanuatu. Prepare to be immersed in a world where tradition is a dynamic force, shaping the present and ensuring the preservation of the Ni-Vanuatu heritage for generations to come.

8.3 Understanding Local Customs and Traditions

For tourists visiting Vanuatu, the journey goes beyond breathtaking landscapes; it extends into the heart of a vibrant culture shaped by centuries of tradition. To make the most of your experience, understanding and respecting local customs and traditions is not just recommended – it's the key to forging genuine connections with the Ni-Vanuatu people.

Everyday Practices and Social Norms

In Vanuatu, life is intricately woven with cultural practices that define the rhythm of daily existence. Greetings hold particular significance; the warm handshake, the gentle nose-to-nose sniff, or a sincere smile are gestures that convey respect and openness. Understanding social norms, such as the communal nature of living and sharing, allows visitors to seamlessly integrate into the fabric of Ni-Vanuatu communities. Embrace the simplicity of everyday rituals, whether it's participating in traditional meals or joining in storytelling sessions beneath the stars.

Traditional Ceremonies and Rituals

Witnessing traditional ceremonies is an immersive way to delve into Vanuatu's rich cultural heritage. Kastom ceremonies, marking significant life events, and yam harvest celebrations, pulsating with energy, offer glimpses into the deep-rooted traditions of the Ni-Vanuatu. As a visitor, observing these events with respect and humility allows you to appreciate the cultural symbolism, intricate dances, and ancient chants that make each ceremony a living testament to the nation's history.

Greetings and Community Bonds

Mastering the art of traditional greetings is a gateway to meaningful interactions. Ni-Vanuatu people are known for their hospitality, and a genuine effort to engage in local greetings fosters a sense of connection. Beyond the surface, recognizing the strength of community bonds reveals the interconnectedness of families and villages. As a guest, acknowledging and participating in these bonds enhances your experience, transforming you from a traveler into an honorary member of the community.

Enhancing Your Journey

Understanding local customs and traditions in Vanuatu is not just a cultural courtesy; it's a pathway to a more enriching and immersive travel experience. By respecting these customs, tourists become contributors to the preservation of Vanuatu's unique identity. The warm reception from the Ni-Vanuatu people becomes more than hospitality; it becomes a shared celebration of culture and a lasting memory of a journey well-treasured.

As you navigate the islands of Vanuatu, keep this cultural compass close, allowing it to guide you through a tapestry of traditions that make every moment in this South Pacific paradise truly unforgettable.

8.4 Souvenirs and Mementos

1. Handwoven Tapa Cloth:

Embrace the artistic craftsmanship of Vanuatu with a handwoven tapa cloth. Created from the inner bark of mulberry trees, these unique textiles feature traditional designs and symbols. Tapa cloths hold cultural significance, often depicting stories and ancestral connections. They make for a meaningful and visually stunning souvenir, perfect for decorating your home or gifting to a special someone.

2. Custom Carved Wooden Artifacts:

Dive into Vanuatu's rich woodcarving tradition by selecting a custom-carved wooden artifact. From intricately carved masks and statues to ceremonial bowls, each piece reflects the skilled artistry of Ni-Vanuatu carvers. These artifacts not only capture the essence of Vanuatu's cultural heritage but also serve as distinctive and authentic reminders of your island adventures.

3. Local Art and Paintings:

Support Vanuatu's burgeoning art scene by bringing home a piece of locally crafted artwork or a vibrant painting. Many talented Ni-Vanuatu artists draw inspiration from their surroundings, creating pieces that showcase the beauty of the islands, traditional ceremonies, and daily life. A painting or sculpture can serve as a colorful and evocative memento of your time in Vanuatu.

4. Kava Bowl and Set:

Immerse yourself in the island's social rituals by acquiring a kava bowl and set. Kava, a traditional and culturally significant drink in Vanuatu, is prepared and shared in communal settings. A beautifully crafted kava bowl, often accompanied by intricately designed cups, provides a tangible connection to this age-old tradition. It's a unique and functional souvenir that can be a conversation starter back home.

5. Island-inspired Jewelry:

Carry a piece of Vanuatu with you wherever you go by choosing island-inspired jewelry. From intricately designed shell necklaces to bracelets made from local materials, Ni-Vanuatu artisans create stunning pieces that capture the spirit of the islands. These accessories not only serve as stylish adornments but also as symbols of the natural beauty and cultural vibrancy of Vanuatu.

CHAPTER NINE

OUTDOOR ACTIVITIES

9.1 Diving and Snorkeling Hotspots

1. Champagne Beach, Espiritu Santo

Nestled on the northeastern coast of Espiritu Santo, the largest island in the Vanuatu archipelago, Champagne Beach is a captivating haven celebrated for its pristine beauty. This idyllic location has earned its name from the effervescent clarity of its waters, creating a mesmerizing backdrop for aquatic exploration. With its fine, powdery sand and transparent sea, Champagne Beach stands as a testament to the unspoiled magnificence of Vanuatu.

As you step onto the shores of Champagne Beach, you're greeted by the gentle rustle of palm trees and the inviting lull of the Pacific Ocean. Snorkelers and divers are treated to a kaleidoscope of marine life beneath the surface, where vibrant coral formations and an array of fish species paint an underwater tapestry. The beach itself offers a tranquil retreat, perfect for relaxation and picnics against the backdrop of azure waters.

2. Hideaway Island, Efate

A short boat journey from the main island of Efate unveils the underwater wonders of Hideaway Island, a marine sanctuary revered for its diverse coral gardens. Accessible from Port Vila, the capital of Vanuatu, this idyllic spot is not only a haven for marine enthusiasts but also home to a unique attraction – an underwater post office. Snorkelers and divers can literally mail a waterproof postcard, creating a memorable experience in the crystal-clear waters surrounding Hideaway Island. This sanctuary offers a harmonious blend of natural beauty and underwater exploration, making it a must-visit destination for those seeking both adventure and tranquility.

3. Million Dollar Point, Espiritu Santo

Located near the town of Luganville on Espiritu Santo, Million Dollar Point is a poignant testament to the aftermath of World War II. This dive site earned its name from the immense value of military equipment and vehicles deliberately sunk into the sea at the war's end. Wreck diving enthusiasts are drawn to this underwater museum, where remnants of jeeps, trucks, and even bulldozers can be explored beneath the surface. The aquatic graveyard of Million Dollar Point offers a unique glimpse into history, making it a compelling destination for those intrigued by both the mysteries of the deep and the echoes of the past.

4. SS President Coolidge, Espiritu Santo

Situated off the coast of Espiritu Santo, the SS President Coolidge is a captivating underwater marvel, beckoning divers to explore the remnants of a once-luxurious ocean liner turned troopship. Recognized as one of the most accessible shipwrecks globally, this sunken giant rests near the town of Luganville, offering a haunting yet enchanting journey through maritime history.

The SS President Coolidge met its watery fate during World War II when it struck a friendly mine. Today, the ship lies submerged, adorned with marine life and shrouded in a silent testament to its storied past. Divers can navigate the expansive wreck, discovering artifacts such as chandeliers, guns, and the iconic porcelain statue of "The Lady." The marine life that now calls the ship home adds an extra layer of intrigue to this underwater museum, making it a must-visit destination for history enthusiasts and diving aficionados alike.

5. Coral Gardens, Tanna Island

Off the southern coast of Tanna Island lies a mesmerizing underwater world known as Coral Gardens. This submerged paradise beckons both snorkelers and divers to explore its unique formations and vibrant marine life. Tanna Island, with its rich cultural heritage and diverse landscapes, extends its allure beneath the waves, offering an immersive experience for those seeking to connect with the ocean's wonders.

Coral Gardens presents a kaleidoscope of colors, with coral formations providing a habitat for an array of marine species. Snorkelers can glide effortlessly over the coral gardens, while divers can delve into the depths to encounter schools of tropical fish, rays, and other fascinating underwater inhabitants. The southern coast of Tanna Island unveils a hidden gem for nature lovers, combining the thrill of underwater exploration with the tranquility of this Pacific island paradise.

6. Moso Island Reef, Efate

Accessible by boat from Port Vila on Efate, Moso Island Reef stands as a testament to the untouched beauty of Vanuatu's underwater landscapes. This pristine coral reef, surrounded by the azure waters of the Pacific, offers a serene escape for snorkelers and divers seeking solitude and natural splendor.

Moso Island Reef boasts a diverse ecosystem, with an abundance of coral species providing shelter to a colorful array of fish. The gentle currents and clear waters make this location ideal for both novice and experienced underwater enthusiasts. As you explore the vibrant marine life and intricate coral formations, the sense of tranquility envelops you, creating an unforgettable aquatic experience just a short boat ride from the bustling capital of Port Vila.

7. Blue Hole, Espiritu Santo

Known for its freshwater wonders, the Blue Hole on Espiritu Santo reveals an unexpected underwater treasure—a captivating underwater cavern that beckons divers into its mysterious depths. Located near Luganville, this site presents a harmonious blend of crystal-clear blue water and the allure of marine exploration.

The Blue Hole's fame originates from its stunning surface, where the deep blue hue of the freshwater contrasts with the surrounding greenery. Beneath the surface lies a hidden world—a cavern with intricate formations and a diverse array of marine life. Divers can descend into the depths, exploring the underwater tunnels and encountering unique species that have made the cavern their home. This fusion of freshwater beauty and underwater discovery makes the Blue Hole a must-visit destination for those seeking a distinctive diving experience in the heart of Espiritu Santo.

9.2 Hiking Trails and Nature Reserves

1. Mount Yasur Trail, Tanna Island

Located on the rugged terrain of Tanna Island, the Mount Yasur Trail offers intrepid hikers an extraordinary journey to the summit of an active volcano. Tanna Island, part of the Vanuatu archipelago, is renowned for its dramatic landscapes, and Mount Yasur stands as a symbol of its fiery beauty. The trail, though demanding, is a pilgrimage for adventurers seeking a unique and unforgettable experience.

As hikers ascend the trail, the panoramic views of the volcanic landscape gradually unfold, revealing the rugged terrain and the vast expanse of the Pacific Ocean beyond. The allure of Mount Yasur lies not only in its challenging ascent but in the opportunity to witness live volcanic activity. At the summit, fiery displays and the rumbling echoes of the earth's power create an awe-inspiring spectacle. The journey to Mount Yasur's summit is a harmonious blend of physical challenge and the raw, natural forces that shape this dynamic island.

2. Matevulu Blue Hole Trail, Espiritu Santo

In the heart of Espiritu Santo, the Matevulu Blue Hole Trail beckons hikers into the embrace of lush tropical forests on a quest leading to one of Vanuatu's most enchanting natural wonders—the Matevulu Blue Hole. As adventurers traverse the trail, the anticipation builds, surrounded by the vibrant greenery of the forest. The climax of the journey is the revelation of the stunning azure waters of the blue hole, a breathtaking sight that seems almost surreal against the backdrop of the verdant surroundings.

The hike to the Matevulu Blue Hole not only promises the visual feast of nature but also offers a refreshing reward at its destination. The crystal-clear waters invite hikers to take a rejuvenating dip, surrounded by the untouched beauty of Espiritu Santo. The Matevulu Blue Hole Trail is a testament to the natural wonders hidden within Vanuatu, providing an immersive experience that captivates the senses and leaves an indelible mark on the soul.

3. Mele Cascades Trail, Efate

A short drive from the bustling capital of Port Vila on Efate, the Mele Cascades Trail invites hikers into the heart of a tropical rainforest, culminating in the breathtaking Mele Cascades waterfall. The journey through the rainforest is a sensory delight, accompanied by the soothing sounds of nature—the chirping of birds, the rustle of leaves, and the gentle flow of the Mele River.

As hikers navigate the well-maintained trail, the anticipation heightens until the grand reveal of the Mele Cascades. The waterfall, surrounded by lush vegetation and vibrant flora, cascades down a series of rock formations, creating a mesmerizing display of natural beauty. The trail's end is not just a destination but a sanctuary—a perfect spot for a refreshing swim beneath the cool waters of the Mele Cascades. The Mele Cascades Trail on Efate encapsulates the essence of Vanuatu's tropical paradise, offering a rejuvenating escape and a visual feast for nature enthusiasts.

4. Millennium Cave Trail, Espiritu Santo

Hidden within the heart of Espiritu Santo, the Millennium Cave Trail stands as a testament to the raw beauty and cultural richness of Vanuatu. This immersive trek leads adventurers through dense rainforests, across river crossings, and past traditional villages, offering a holistic experience that delves into both the natural and cultural heritage of the island.

The journey unfolds as hikers navigate the lush rainforest, guided by the symphony of exotic bird calls and the gentle rush of flowing rivers. Along the way, encounters with local villages provide a glimpse into the traditional way of life, creating a cultural tapestry that intertwines seamlessly with the natural surroundings. As the trail progresses, the highlight emerges—the awe-inspiring Millennium Cave. This colossal cavern, adorned with ancient stalactites and stalagmites, captivates the imagination and serves as a living testament to the geological wonders that have shaped the landscape over centuries.

The Millennium Cave Trail is not just a physical expedition; it's a spiritual and sensory journey that immerses hikers in the rich tapestry of Vanuatu's past and present. It's an exploration of the symbiotic relationship between nature and culture, providing an unparalleled experience that lingers in the memory long after the trek is complete.

5. Port Resolution to Sulphur Bay Trail, Tanna Island

Trekking across Tanna Island from Port Resolution to Sulphur Bay unveils a narrative of contrasting landscapes and natural wonders. This trail is a microcosm of Tanna's diverse scenery, showcasing the island's volcanic plains, dense vegetation, and sweeping coastal views. As hikers traverse the path, they witness the striking dichotomy between the ash-covered surroundings of the mighty Mount Yasur and the serene beauty of Sulphur Bay.

The journey begins amid the remnants of volcanic activity, with the blackened soil beneath the footfalls of hikers telling the story of Tanna's geological history. Moving through lush vegetation, the trail eventually reveals expansive coastal panoramas, providing a picturesque vantage point to absorb the island's coastal splendor. The trek encapsulates Tanna's natural diversity, making it a captivating exploration that encapsulates the island's contrasting landscapes and showcases the resilience of life in the face of volcanic forces.

6. Ratua Private Island Trail, Ratua Island

Nestled just off the coast of Espiritu Santo, Ratua Island beckons with a trail that meanders through coconut plantations, lush forests, and pristine beaches. This exclusive hiking experience on Ratua Island offers more than just a physical journey; it's a seamless blend of natural beauty and luxury on a private island sanctuary.

Trails wind through coconut groves, where the rustle of palm leaves accompanies hikers through the heart of the island's tropical paradise. The scent of the sea mingles with the fragrance of blooming flowers as the trail opens up to secluded beaches with untouched sands and turquoise waters. The journey on Ratua Island is an invitation to unwind in nature's embrace, where the serenity of the surroundings creates a tranquil escape from the demands of everyday life. This exclusive trail is a testament to the harmonious coexistence of pristine landscapes and luxurious retreats on Ratua Island, offering a hiking experience that seamlessly fuses natural beauty with opulent seclusion.

9.3 Waterfall Exploration and Eco-Tours

Embark on a journey of discovery as we guide you through the mesmerizing world of Vanuatu's waterfalls, where nature's beauty and cultural significance intertwine.

Unveiling Hidden Gems

The allure of Vanuatu's waterfalls lies not only in their visual splendor but also in the cultural stories they hold. From the pristine jungles of Espiritu Santo to the verdant landscapes of Tanna Island, each waterfall has its own unique character and significance within the local communities. This section serves as a compass, leading you to the hidden gems where cascading waters tell tales of the land's history and traditions.

Guided Tours and Responsible Exploration

To truly appreciate the magic of Vanuatu's waterfalls, consider joining guided tours that not only showcase the natural beauty but also emphasize responsible tourism practices. Knowledgeable guides provide insights into the local flora and fauna, as well as the cultural importance of these water features. These tours are designed to leave minimal impact on the environment, ensuring that future generations can continue to marvel at the wonders of Vanuatu.

Eco-Tours and Sustainability

Vanuatu takes pride in its commitment to sustainability, and eco-tours focused on waterfall exploration exemplify this dedication. These tours are designed to minimize the ecological footprint by adhering to principles of environmental conservation. Through educational initiatives, participants gain an understanding of the delicate ecosystems surrounding the waterfalls and learn how their presence can contribute positively to the preservation of these pristine environments.

Sustainable Travel Practices

As you embark on your waterfall adventure, consider adopting sustainable travel practices to further minimize your impact. Support local businesses that prioritize eco-friendly initiatives, and choose accommodations committed to responsible tourism. By engaging in activities that respect the environment and local communities, you become an advocate for the preservation of Vanuatu's natural treasures.

Contribution to Preservation

Vanuatu's waterfalls are not just picturesque attractions; they are integral to the ecological balance and cultural identity of the islands. This section guides you on how you can actively contribute to their preservation. Whether through participating in community-led conservation projects, adhering to Leave No Trace principles, or supporting initiatives that promote sustainable tourism, you play a crucial role in ensuring that these cascading wonders remain untouched by the negative impacts of mass tourism.

The Tranquility of Cascading Waters

Get ready to be captivated by the sheer beauty and tranquility of Vanuatu's cascading waterfalls. Imagine the rhythmic sounds of water meeting rock, the refreshing mist on your face, and the vibrant greenery that surrounds these natural wonders. Through responsible exploration and an appreciation for the cultural significance of these sites, you not only embark on a memorable adventure but become a steward of Vanuatu's ecological and cultural heritage. As you chase waterfalls in this Pacific paradise, let the experience be a harmonious blend of awe, respect, and a commitment to preserving the serenity of these pristine environments for generations to come.

CHAPTER TEN

VANUATU TRAVEL ITINERARIES

10.1 One-Week Highlights Tour

For those with limited time but an insatiable wanderlust, our specially curated one-week highlights tour is the key to unlocking the best of Vanuatu's treasures. In this chapter, we present a detailed itinerary that promises an unforgettable journey, guiding you through must-see attractions and cultural gems scattered across the archipelago.

Day 1-2: Port Vila's Vibrant Markets and Cultural Delights

Your adventure begins in the lively capital of Vanuatu, Port Vila. Nestled along the shores of Efate Island, this bustling town sets the stage for an immersive cultural experience. Spend your first day exploring the vibrant markets, where the kaleidoscope of colors, fragrances, and local crafts offers a glimpse into daily life.

As the sun sets, indulge in a feast of local delicacies at one of the waterfront restaurants. Immerse yourself in the rhythms of traditional music and dance, an integral part of Ni-Vanuatu culture. The next day, venture into the hinterlands to discover hidden waterfalls and lush landscapes, providing a serene contrast to the lively atmosphere of Port Vila.

Day 3-4: Espiritu Santo's Aquatic Paradise

Fly to Espiritu Santo, known as the 'Largest Island' and a haven for water enthusiasts. Spend your third day snorkeling in the crystalline waters of the famous Blue Hole, a natural wonder surrounded by lush rainforest. Explore the underwater world teeming with vibrant marine life, coral gardens, and the remnants of World War II wrecks.

On the fourth day, embark on a journey to Champagne Beach, renowned for its powdery white sands and crystal-clear waters. Relax under the swaying palm trees, take a dip in the azure sea, and savor a beachside picnic. The tranquility of Santo provides a serene escape, allowing you to recharge before the next leg of your adventure.

Day 5-6: Tanna's Volcanic Wonders and Cultural Immersion

A short flight takes you to Tanna, an island where ancient traditions and natural wonders coexist harmoniously. Witness the awe-inspiring Mt. Yasur, one of the world's most accessible active volcanoes. Feel the earth beneath you tremble as molten lava lights up the night sky—an unforgettable experience that connects you with the raw power of nature.

Day six invites you to delve into Tanna's rich cultural tapestry. Visit traditional villages, where friendly locals welcome you with open arms. Participate in age-old ceremonies, taste local cuisine prepared with ancestral recipes, and gain insights into the spiritual beliefs that shape the islanders' way of life. Tanna offers a rare blend of adventure and cultural immersion that lingers in your memories.

Day 7: Farewell to Paradise

As your one-week highlights tour concludes, take a moment to reflect on the myriad experiences that have colored your journey through Vanuatu. Depart from Tanna with a heart full of memories and a camera filled with snapshots of this South Pacific paradise.

This specially curated itinerary ensures that every moment of your week-long adventure is optimized for discovery and enjoyment. From the bustling markets of Port Vila to the serene beaches of Espiritu Santo and the volcanic wonders of Tanna, each day brings a new dimension to your Vanuatu experience. Pack your sense of wonder and readiness for adventure; Vanuatu awaits your exploration.

10.2 Two-Week Grand Tour

For the intrepid traveler yearning for a more profound connection with the South Pacific paradise of Vanuatu, the two-week grand tour stands as an enticing prospect. This carefully crafted expedition beckons you to immerse yourself in the rich tapestry of Vanuatu's diverse islands, promising an exploration that goes beyond the surface. In the next thousand words, we invite you to embark on a journey that delves deep into the heart of Vanuatu's beauty, culture, and untouched landscapes.

Days 1-3: Arrival in Port Vila and Introduction to Vanuatu's Culture

As you touch down in Port Vila, the vibrant capital city, the grand tour begins. Spend your initial days acclimating to the rhythm of Vanuatu, where the warm hospitality of the locals sets the tone for the adventures ahead. Explore the bustling markets, where the aroma of tropical fruits mingles with the vibrant colors of local handicrafts. Engage with the Ni-Vanuatu people, eager to share their stories and traditions.

On the third day, venture into the heart of Port Vila's cultural scene. Visit museums that house artifacts revealing the island nation's history, and attend traditional performances that showcase the dynamic dance and music integral to Vanuatu's identity. As the sun sets, dine on local delicacies at a seaside restaurant, your senses absorbing the essence of Vanuatu's capital.

Days 4-6: Espiritu Santo's Aquatic Wonderland

Board a flight to Espiritu Santo, the largest of Vanuatu's islands, where an aquatic wonderland awaits. Over the next three days, dive into the azure waters surrounding Santo, discovering the treasures that lie beneath. Snorkel through the famed Blue Hole, an otherworldly sinkhole surrounded by lush rainforest, and explore the vibrant marine life that thrives in this underwater sanctuary.

Continue your aquatic adventure by visiting the world-renowned Million Dollar Point, where the remnants of World War II lie submerged—a testament to the island's historical significance. Conclude your time in Santo with a visit to Champagne Beach, where the crystalline waters and pristine shores provide the ideal backdrop for relaxation and reflection.

Days 7-9: Ambrym's Mystical Rainforests and Cultural Encounters

From Santo, a short flight takes you to Ambrym, an island shrouded in mystique. For the next three days, traverse Ambrym's lush rainforests on invigorating hikes that unveil the island's untouched beauty. Encounter rare flora and fauna, and breathe in the earthy scents of the ancient forests that have stood the test of time.

In the heart of Ambrym, immerse yourself in the island's unique culture. Witness traditional ceremonies performed by local tribes, where ancient rituals come to life through dance, music, and intricate body paintings. Engage with the villagers, gaining insight into their spiritual beliefs and daily lives. Ambrym offers a genuine and unfiltered connection with Vanuatu's indigenous heritage.

Days 10-12: Tanna's Volcanic Majesty and Cultural Abundance

A short flight transports you to Tanna, where the majestic Mt. Yasur, an active volcano, dominates the landscape. Spend the next three days exploring the volatile wonders of Tanna, standing in awe as molten lava paints the night sky. Tanna's volcanic landscapes provide a stark contrast to its vibrant cultural scene.

Delve into the intricacies of Tanna's cultural tapestry by visiting remote villages. Engage with locals, partake in traditional ceremonies, and savor authentic cuisine prepared with generations-old recipes. The juxtaposition of Tanna's natural wonders and cultural richness creates an experience that transcends the ordinary, leaving an indelible mark on your journey through Vanuatu.

Days 13-14: Farewell to Vanuatu

As the grand tour concludes, spend your final days reflecting on the myriad experiences that have defined your two-week odyssey through Vanuatu. Depart from Tanna with a deep appreciation for the diversity that defines this island nation—a spectrum of landscapes, cultures, and traditions that collectively paint the portrait of Vanuatu's unparalleled allure.

The two-week grand tour is a testament to the richness and complexity of Vanuatu's offerings. It goes beyond the conventional tourist experience, allowing you to not only witness but also deeply engage with the multifaceted layers of this South Pacific gem.

10.3 Family-Friendly Adventure

This day-by-day itinerary is crafted to guide you through a weeklong journey that seamlessly blends excitement, education, and relaxation for every member of the family. From the bustling markets of Port Vila to the serene beaches of Espiritu Santo and the cultural richness of Tanna, each day promises new discoveries and shared moments.

Day 1: Arrival in Port Vila and Cultural Immersion

Morning: Arrive in Port Vila, the capital of Vanuatu, where the warmth of the locals welcomes you. Check into your family-friendly accommodation, strategically chosen for its amenities catering to all ages.

Afternoon: Dive into the cultural heart of Vanuatu with a visit to the Port Vila Markets. Let the kids explore the vibrant stalls filled with local crafts, tropical fruits, and colorful souvenirs. Engage with the friendly vendors and savor your first taste of Vanuatu's rich culture.

Evening: Enjoy a family dinner at a waterfront restaurant, where the gentle sea breeze accompanies traditional music and dance performances. The evening sets the tone for a week filled with cultural immersion and shared experiences.

Day 2: Exploring Port Vila's Natural Beauty

Morning: Embark on a family-friendly nature walk to Mele Cascades. The easy trail through lush rainforest leads to a stunning waterfall, where everyone can cool off with a refreshing swim.

Afternoon: Head to Ekasup Cultural Village for an interactive cultural experience. Participate in traditional dances, witness ancient ceremonies, and learn about the customs and traditions that define Vanuatu.

Evening: Cap off the day with a relaxing family dinner at a local eatery, sharing stories of the day's adventures.

Day 3: Island Hopping to Hideaway Island

Morning: Take a short boat ride to Hideaway Island, a marine sanctuary with pristine coral reefs. Snorkel in the clear waters and marvel at the vibrant underwater world. The calm conditions make it an ideal spot for families to explore together.

Afternoon: Enjoy a picnic lunch on the island and engage in water activities suitable for all ages, from paddleboarding to kayaking. Capture family moments against the backdrop of turquoise waters and swaying palm trees.

Evening: Return to Port Vila for a leisurely evening. Explore the local nightlife or unwind at your accommodation's family-friendly facilities.

Day 4: Flight to Espiritu Santo - Blue Hole Adventure

Morning: Fly to Espiritu Santo, the largest island in Vanuatu. Check into your family-friendly resort, strategically chosen for its proximity to Blue Hole, one of Santo's natural wonders.

Afternoon: Spend the afternoon at the famous Blue Hole, a natural swimming pool surrounded by lush rainforest. The clear blue waters provide a safe and magical environment for families to enjoy swimming and snorkeling.

Evening: Relish a family dinner at your resort, sharing stories of the day's exploration.

Day 5: Beach Bliss at Champagne Beach

Morning: Journey to Champagne Beach, renowned for its powder-soft white sand and crystal-clear waters. Relax under the shade of palm trees and build sandcastles with the kids.

Afternoon: Enjoy a beachside picnic and partake in family-friendly water activities. The calm and shallow nature of the water makes it ideal for young swimmers.

Evening: As the sun sets over Champagne Beach, revel in a beachfront family dinner or explore local eateries for a taste of Santo's culinary delights.

Day 6: Wildlife Encounters and Family-Friendly Trails in Santo

Morning: Explore Santo's flora and fauna at the Santo Horse Adventures and Farmstay. Engage in family-friendly activities such as horse riding, interacting with farm animals, and discovering the biodiversity of the island.

Afternoon: Head to Loru Conservation Area for a family-friendly hike through lush rainforests. Discover hidden waterfalls and learn about the island's unique ecosystems.

Evening: Conclude the day with a family dinner, sharing the highlights of your wildlife encounters and nature walks.

Day 7: Tanna's Volcanic Majesty and Cultural Immersion

Morning: Fly to Tanna, known for its active volcano, Mt. Yasur. Check into your family-friendly accommodation, strategically chosen for its comfort and proximity to Tanna's attractions.

Afternoon: Visit Mt. Yasur and witness the awe-inspiring volcanic activity. The experience of seeing molten lava lighting up the night sky creates a lasting memory for every family member.

Evening: Engage in a cultural exchange with locals in a traditional village. Participate in ceremonies, taste local cuisine, and gain insight into Tanna's rich cultural heritage.

Day 8: Departure from Tanna - Farewell to Vanuatu

Morning: Spend your final morning in Tanna reflecting on the incredible experiences of the week. Visit any local attractions or markets you may have missed.

Afternoon: Bid farewell to Tanna as you board your flight back home, leaving with hearts full of memories and a shared family adventure that transcends the ordinary.

This weeklong family-friendly adventure in Vanuatu is a carefully curated journey that balances exploration, relaxation, and cultural immersion. Each day offers a new facet of Vanuatu's charm, creating an unforgettable experience for every family member. Whether snorkeling in Port Vila's crystal-clear waters, exploring Santo's natural wonders, or witnessing the majesty of Tanna's volcano, this itinerary ensures that every moment is cherished and the bonds of family are strengthened against the backdrop of Vanuatu's unparalleled beauty.

10.4 Solo Traveler's Journey

Embarking on a solo journey to Vanuatu offers a unique opportunity for self-discovery, adventure, and cultural immersion. This meticulously crafted 7-day itinerary takes you through the diverse landscapes and rich cultural tapestry of the archipelago, ensuring that every day is filled with meaningful experiences that cater to the solo traveler's desire for exploration and introspection.

Day 1: Arrival in Port Vila - Embracing Island Vibes

Your solo adventure begins as you touch down in Port Vila, the vibrant capital of Vanuatu. Start your journey by immersing yourself in the island vibes. Check into a centrally located accommodation, offering both comfort and proximity to the town's attractions. Spend the day strolling along the waterfront, exploring local markets, and sampling traditional cuisine at a waterfront restaurant. Engage with locals and fellow travelers, setting the tone for the cultural exchange that will define your solo odyssey.

Day 2: Cultural Dive in Port Vila - Museums and Local Experiences

Delve into the cultural richness of Vanuatu on your second day. Visit the Vanuatu Cultural Centre, where exhibits showcase the history, art, and traditions of the islands. Attend traditional performances that bring the vibrant stories of Vanuatu to life. In the afternoon, embark on a self-guided tour of Port Vila's street art, discovering the murals that depict the island's cultural heritage. As the day concludes, dine at a local eatery, savoring the flavors of Vanuatu's diverse cuisine.

Day 3: Espiritu Santo - Snorkeling in the Blue Hole

Fly to Espiritu Santo, where the third day brings an aquatic adventure. Explore the famed Blue Hole, a natural wonder surrounded by lush rainforest. Snorkel in its crystal-clear waters, marveling at the underwater world teeming with colorful marine life. In the evening, relax on the pristine Champagne Beach, known for its powdery white sands and breathtaking sunset views. Connect with fellow travelers at a beachside gathering, sharing stories of your solo escapades.

Day 4: Espiritu Santo - Nature Walks and Historical Exploration

Engage in nature walks on your fourth day in Santo. Explore the hidden waterfalls and verdant landscapes that make Espiritu Santo a haven for nature enthusiasts. In the afternoon, visit Million Dollar Point, an underwater museum of World War II relics. Discover the historical significance of the artifacts submerged in the crystalline waters. As the day winds down, relish the tranquility of Santo's natural wonders, finding solace in the simplicity of the surroundings.

Day 5: Ambrym - Volcanic Wonders and Cultural Immersion

Catch a flight to Ambrym, a mystical island where volcanic landscapes and ancient traditions converge. Spend the day hiking to the rim of Mt. Benbow or Mt. Marum, experiencing the raw power of Vanuatu's active volcanoes. In the evening, engage with local communities, witnessing traditional ceremonies that offer a glimpse into the spiritual beliefs of the islanders. Enjoy a night under the starry sky, the glow of the volcanic activity casting an otherworldly ambiance.

Day 6: Ambrym - Exploring Villages and Artisanal Crafts

On your sixth day, explore the villages of Ambrym, where local artisans create traditional handicrafts. Engage in hands-on experiences, learning the art of sand drawing and wood carving. Participate in communal activities, fostering connections with the friendly inhabitants. As the day unfolds, appreciate the simplicity of Ambrym's way of life and the warmth of its people.

Day 7: Tanna - Mt. Yasur and Farewell to Vanuatu

Conclude your solo journey with a flight to Tanna, home to the awe-inspiring Mt. Yasur. Spend your final day hiking to the crater's edge, where the spectacular display of molten lava against the night sky leaves an indelible mark on your Vanuatu adventure. As you bid farewell to the islands, take with you the memories of a solo journey filled with exploration, cultural immersion, and the untamed beauty of Vanuatu.

This 7-day itinerary for the solo traveler encapsulates the essence of Vanuatu—a journey that transcends the ordinary, allowing you to connect with nature, engage with diverse cultures, and create a narrative of self-discovery. From the bustling markets of Port Vila to the volcanic majesty of Tanna, each day unfolds a new chapter in your solo odyssey, promising an adventure that lingers in your heart long after you leave the South Pacific paradise.

10.5 Romantic Getaways

For couples seeking a perfect blend of tranquility, adventure, and romance, Vanuatu offers an enchanting backdrop for an unforgettable romantic getaway. This day-by-day itinerary is meticulously crafted to immerse you in the idyllic beauty of the South Pacific, fostering moments of intimacy, exploration, and relaxation that will linger in your hearts forever.

Day 1: Arrival in Port Vila - Love by the Waterfront

Your romantic escapade begins in Port Vila, the capital city of Vanuatu. Upon arrival, let the tropical breeze and warm welcomes set the tone for your journey. Check into a luxurious beachfront resort, where the azure waters of the Pacific provide a breathtaking view from your private accommodation. Enjoy a leisurely afternoon by the pool or on the beach, soaking in the serenity of your surroundings.

As the sun sets, embark on a romantic stroll along the waterfront. The bustling markets transform into a romantic haven, with local musicians playing soulful melodies and vendors offering delicious street food. Choose a waterfront restaurant for an intimate dinner, savoring the flavors of Vanuatu's fresh seafood and local delicacies.

Day 2: Discovering Mele Cascades - Nature's Embrace

Start your day with a hearty breakfast before heading to Mele Cascades, a mesmerizing waterfall surrounded by lush rainforest. Take a leisurely walk through the tropical foliage, hand in hand, until you reach the cascading waters. Cool off with a refreshing swim in the natural pools beneath the falls, creating memories of shared laughter and moments of quiet bliss.

In the afternoon, return to Port Vila and indulge in a couples' massage at a spa overlooking the ocean. Let the expert hands of local therapists melt away any lingering tension, leaving you both rejuvenated and ready for the romantic adventures that lie ahead.

Day 3: Island-Hopping to Hideaway Island - Underwater Love

Embark on an island-hopping adventure to Hideaway Island, a pristine marine sanctuary known for its crystal-clear waters and vibrant coral reefs. Explore the underwater world hand in hand, snorkeling amidst colorful fish and coral formations. Take a moment to send a postcard from the world's only underwater post office, creating a unique memento of your romantic escapade.

Return to your resort for a quiet evening, perhaps with a private dinner on the beach or in the comfort of your villa. Revel in the sounds of the ocean as you share a bottle of local wine and toast to the love that brought you to this tropical paradise.

Day 4: Flight to Tanna - Sunset at White Grass Ocean Resort

Fly to Tanna, where the dramatic landscapes and cultural richness set the stage for the next chapter of your romantic journey. Check into the White Grass Ocean Resort, perched on a hillside with panoramic views of the Pacific. Spend the afternoon unwinding in your private bungalow or exploring the resort's lush gardens hand in hand.

As the sun begins to dip below the horizon, embark on a sunset tour to Mount Yasur, one of the world's most accessible active volcanoes. Witness the fiery display of molten lava against the night sky, creating a mesmerizing and unforgettable moment for you and your loved one.

Day 5: Cultural Immersion in Tanna - Bonding with Local Traditions

Delve into the cultural richness of Tanna with a visit to traditional villages. Engage with the friendly locals, participate in age-old ceremonies, and witness dances that tell the stories of the island's history. Share a traditional meal with a local family, savoring the flavors of Vanuatu while connecting with the heart of Tanna's culture.

In the evening, return to your resort and indulge in a private candlelit dinner under the stars. The tranquil setting and the warmth of the Tanna night sky provide an intimate backdrop for a romantic evening.

Day 6: Relaxation and Reflection - Tanna's Natural Delights

Take a leisurely morning to relax and reflect on the experiences of the past days. Enjoy a couples' spa treatment or simply lounge by the pool, surrounded by the natural beauty of Tanna. In the afternoon, venture to the picturesque Lowinio Beach for a serene and romantic beach picnic.

As the sun sets on your final evening in Tanna, savor a farewell dinner at the resort's restaurant, celebrating the memories you've created and the love that has deepened amidst the beauty of Vanuatu.

Day 7: Departure from Paradise - Carrying Love Beyond the Islands

As your romantic getaway comes to an end, depart Tanna with a heart full of cherished memories. Take one last glance at the landscapes that have witnessed the love and connection shared during your time in Vanuatu. Board your flight with a promise to return, knowing that the love cultivated in this South Pacific paradise will forever be a part of your story.

In conclusion, this day-by-day itinerary for a romantic getaway in Vanuatu is crafted to immerse couples in the beauty, culture, and intimacy that define this tropical paradise.

Note: Depending on your travel goals as stated in chapter one of this travel guide and the type of travel itinerary you would like to go for, you can still add some places you would like to visit which were not included in your choice travel itinerary, you can adjust any of them to suit your travel goals so as to a have an enjoyable and memorable trip.

CHAPTER ELEVEN

PRACTICAL TIPS AND RESOURCES

11.1 Local Phrases and Vocabulary

Bislama is the national language, and while English and French are also widely spoken, here are some key phrases and vocabulary to help you connect with the vibrant culture of Vanuatu:

Greetings:

- Hello - Halo
- Good morning - Gud moning
- Good afternoon - Gud aftonun
- Good evening - Gud nait

Common Expressions:

- Thank you - Tangkyu tumas
- Yes - Ya
- No - Nae
- Please - Plis
- Excuse me - Skius mi
- I'm sorry - Sori tumas

Getting Around:

- Where is...? - Wea hemi...?
- How much is this? - Hem i stap hao mase?
- I need help - Mi nidim help

- Where is the bathroom? - Wea hemi garem batrum?

Food and Dining:

- Delicious - Hemia smol tumas!
- What is this called? - Hem i kat wanem nem?
- I would like... - Mi wantem...
- The bill, please - Bil blong mi, plis

Cultural Interactions:

- What is your name? - Wanem nem blong yu?
- My name is... - Nem blong mi hemi...
- Nice to meet you - Mi glad tumas long miting yu
- How are you? - Yu stap gut?

Nature and Environment:

- Beach - Bich
- Mountain - Maonten
- Waterfall - Wotaful
- Island - Ailan

Feel free to use these phrases as a starting point to connect with the friendly people of Vanuatu. The locals will appreciate your efforts to embrace their language and culture.

11.2 Emergency Contacts

Familiarize yourself with the following emergency contacts to ensure a prompt and effective response in times of need:

1. Police Emergency:

- Contact Number: 112 or 111
- The Vanuatu Police Force is available to assist with any safety or security concerns. Whether you encounter a local issue or need police intervention, dialing 112 or 111 will connect you to emergency services.

2. Medical Assistance:

- Vila Central Hospital (Port Vila): +678 22666
- Northern District Hospital (Santo): +678 37633
- In case of a medical emergency, these hospitals are equipped to provide essential healthcare services. For urgent medical attention, contact the relevant hospital and seek assistance.

Fire and Rescue:

- Fire Emergency: 115
- While fire emergencies are rare, it's crucial to have the contact number for the fire department. Dial 115 in the event of a fire or related emergencies requiring immediate attention.

Australian High Commission (Port Vila):

- Emergency Consular Assistance: +678 22777
- For Australian tourists, the Australian High Commission in Port Vila provides emergency consular assistance. Save this number for any consular support you may need during your stay.

New Zealand High Commission (Port Vila):

- Emergency Assistance: +678 22129
- New Zealand tourists can reach out to the New Zealand High Commission in Port Vila for emergency assistance. This contact is valuable for consular support during your visit.

Natural Disaster Hotline: 111 or 115

Vanuatu is prone to natural disasters such as cyclones. Stay informed about local conditions and contact the natural disaster hotline in case of any imminent threat or emergency related to adverse weather conditions.

11.3 Health Precautions

To ensure a safe and healthy journey, consider the following health precautions:

1. Vaccinations and Health Checks:

Ensure routine vaccinations are up-to-date, including measles, mumps, rubella, and diphtheria. Check with your healthcare provider for recommendations on additional vaccines such as hepatitis A and B. It's advisable to have a general health check before traveling.

2, Sun Protection:

Vanuatu enjoys a tropical climate, and the sun can be intense. Pack and regularly apply a high SPF sunscreen, wear protective clothing, and consider a wide-brimmed hat and sunglasses to shield yourself from the sun's rays.

3. Stay Hydrated:

With warm temperatures and outdoor activities, staying hydrated is crucial. Drink plenty of bottled or filtered water, especially if engaging in physical activities like hiking or snorkeling.

4. Insect Protection:

Vanuatu is in a malaria-risk zone, so consult your healthcare provider about appropriate antimalarial medication before your trip. Additionally, use insect repellent to guard against mosquito bites, especially during the evenings.

5. Local Water and Food Safety:

Stick to bottled or filtered water to avoid waterborne illnesses. Be cautious with street food and ensure that any fruits and vegetables are thoroughly washed or peeled before consumption.

6. First Aid Kit:

Pack a basic first aid kit with essentials such as adhesive bandages, antiseptic wipes, pain relievers, and any necessary prescription medications. It's always better to be prepared for minor injuries or ailments.

7. Emergency Medical Services:

Familiarize yourself with the location of the nearest medical facilities in the areas you plan to visit. Keep a list of emergency contacts, including local hospitals and the contact information for your country's embassy or consulate.

Remember that individual health needs may vary, so it's advisable to consult with a healthcare professional well before your trip. Taking these precautions will help ensure a healthy and enjoyable stay in Vanuatu.

Made in the USA
Monee, IL
17 December 2024

995303a2-ec42-4270-a990-6985ad69273eR01